IMMOVABLE
HEART
UNSTOPPABLE
MIND

A PERSONAL GUIDE TO THE
6 ESSENTIAL PRACTICES
FOR LIVING A HEALTHY AND
FULFILLING LIFE

DAVID ZAPPASODI

Author Photo © Aaron Dressin Photography

ISBN: 1503212769
ISBN 13: 9781503212763
Library of Congress Control Number: 2014920503
CreateSpace Independent Publishing Platform
North Charleston, South Carolina

This book is for my wife, Cara.
You are my best friend and my greatest teacher,
and I love you with all of my heart.

This book is also for those who are struggling
and feel stuck with their health goals.
Let's see what we can do about this…

TABLE OF CONTENTS

ACKNOWLEDGEMENTS

I would like to offer my deepest gratitude for all the support, guidance and love I have received throughout the process of writing this book. Without the help of some very special people in my life, it certainly wouldn't have been possible.

To my parents, Kathy and David Zappasodi, thank you not only for the gift of this life, but for your unconditional love and support throughout all of it. Anytime I've needed a helping hand or a listening ear, I've always known I can turn to you.

To my good friend and editor, Daye Proffit, thank you for approaching me after one of my presentations and inspiring me to write this book. I also thank you for your discerning eye, attention to detail, and valuable guidance throughout the entire editing process. I feel very fortunate that you have come into my life, and that I get to work closely with you.

To Dale and Vanessa Munger, you are amazing examples of generosity and have been such great friends to Cara and me. Thank you for all your love and support; we are blessed to know you.

A heartfelt thanks goes out to Theresa Spinello Aliotta, Carolyn Pole, Tiffany Hall, Tina Fitzgerald, and my brother Brian Zappasodi for reading through the manuscript and giving me helpful feedback and suggestions. Also, a special thanks goes out to Aaron Dressin for your incredible photography and beautiful spirit.

To my Mother-In-Law, Diane Beall, thank you for always being there for me and Cara, and for being so involved – coming to my presentations, reading through the material, and giving me your thoughts on various aspects of it. You have been very helpful in the process of this book coming together, and I am very grateful to have you in my life.

To my teacher, Mitra Bishop-Roshi, thank you for your compassionate wisdom and for being such a shining example of all the practices described in this book. You've helped me to have a greater faith that there is, indeed, more to who we are than there appears to be.

Lastly, to my wife, Cara, I could write a whole book on all the love and support you've given me over the years. We've had great times and challenging times, and we've grown stronger and more connected through all of it. I am so grateful and honored to be on this journey with you.

INVITATION

Hello my friend,

I want to begin this book by letting you know that I have a vision, and that *you* are a part of it. That's right – you! You see, you and I are intimately connected. In this wide and expansive universe, you and I are both right here next to each other, living on a tiny ball of land and water that is flying through a vast ocean of empty space, and we are sharing in this human experience together. Yet despite our connection, we are capable of believing that we are separate from each other. We have brought about all kinds of problems for ourselves, and our planet, because of this belief – including our "health" problems.

The time for believing that we are separate from each other is coming to an end. A new vision is arising – a vision that includes not just an elite few, but all of us:

My vision is to cultivate a healthy and fulfilling life, not just for myself but for my whole human family, through an approach that brings abundance, connection, growth, joy, and freedom – for the benefit of all.

I am committed to living this vision, because it's the most amazing one I can imagine living. Billions of people all over the world are unhealthy and unhappy, they are suffering and they are searching for answers desperately. The abundance of information available doesn't seem to be making a dent in the problem, and neither do the commonly held beliefs that we hold to be true about health. Rather than be modest, I must be honest – I truly believe that this book will contribute to improving the health of humanity. It is a movement toward simplicity, toward the essence of what health really is, and it is a book that applies to all of us, regardless of our current conditions.

If you would like to live a more healthy and fulfilling life, I am reaching to you with a helping hand. I am not reaching as someone that wants to fix you, because you don't need to be fixed. I am reaching out my hand as a friend that wants to be more connected with you. I invite you to take it.

INTRODUCTION

"I'm paying you $60 an hour, and coming to see you three times a week, so you better get me the results I want."

I started my health career as a personal trainer, and this was a very common statement I would hear from my clients. Like many other personal trainers, I felt a great pressure to make sure my clients achieved their goals. They were, after all, investing a lot of money into me, and the knowledge I had about health and wellness, so it seemed to make sense that I would be responsible for their progress.

I've always done pretty well under pressure, so when I started to feel it coming from my clients, it gave me a sense of determination, and I began to dive deep into educating myself. Of course, educating myself didn't just mean studying; it meant applying what I learned as well. So, for many years I experimented with a multitude of exercise styles and nutrition programs, both on myself and on my clients.

The conclusion? With all the things I tried, I found that regardless of the exercise style or nutrition program I used, a few people got results, but the majority of people didn't. This wasn't exactly surprising, given that the vast majority of people in the U.S. don't reach their health goals, and each year our country is the most unhealthy it has ever been. Still, I've always expected more from myself, so what all my efforts helped me to realize was that the solution to our health problems was not going to be found in one specific modality. Different people do well with different styles of exercise and nutrition, and because of this, there is no one specific exercise or food that everyone will do well with.

This realization brought me to my next area of focus – individualization. For years I dove into various physical assessment protocols that helped me create exercise programs for each person's specific needs. I learned to test people's metabolism, and give them nutritional recommendations based on their biochemistry. Still, with all the individualization in my program designs, what I found was essentially the same – some people got good results, but the majority of people didn't. I slowly realized over time that individualization is not the ultimate solution to our health problems either. There was still something I was missing.

During all these years of study and experimentation, I was also looking for any patterns I could find in the people that were successful with their goals, as well as in those who were not. This eventually got me interested in mindset, and how it influences our progress. For example, one of the things I noticed was that most people were more focused on moving away from what they didn't want, rather than moving toward what they did want. For example, when I asked, "Why do you want to lose weight?" most people would tell me about how they were tired of feeling gross or unattractive, or sick of seeing themselves in the mirror, or fed up with being uncomfortable or struggling to function in some way. Their answers told me, very clearly, what they *didn't* want anymore, but they didn't tell me what they *did* want. However, when I asked them, "If we got rid of all these things, what would your life be like?" the most common answer I got was a blank stare, followed by "I don't know." It amazed me that they had never thought to ask themselves that question, or realize how important it was in influencing their progress.

Another pattern I noticed was that our inner lives and outer lives are reflective of each other. I was able to see this pattern after being inspired by a quote from the Bible, and making it a huge part of my own spiritual practice. It's the one about not trying to take the dust out of my brother's eye, and instead focusing on removing the log from my own. What I came to realize after contemplating this message and practicing it on a daily basis, is that we are completely responsible for our life, and the extent to which we are not willing to take responsibility for it is the extent to which we are not empowered. Anything that we perceive in the outside world is coming to us through the filter of our own minds, which is why two people can witness the same event and have completely different perspectives on what happened. So everything we experience, whether pleasing or disturbing, is a reflection of us in some way. It may not be readily apparent, but we can always find the connection if we only look deeply enough. And unbelievable growth can occur when we do.

So how does all this apply to health? Well, for one thing, it helped me to realize how counterproductive it was for me to believe that I was responsible for someone else's progress. I started having much deeper relationships with my clients after realizing this. It also gave me other avenues of approach that I didn't have before. For example, I once worked with a woman who wanted to lose about 60 pounds. She worked hard and did everything I asked her to, but no matter how hard she worked or how much I changed her program, her weight wouldn't budge. I was getting pretty frustrated, because I couldn't figure out why we weren't making progress. So when she came in one day for her personal training session, I told her that I wasn't going to train her that day. Instead, I wanted to sit down and talk with her for a while. We talked for an hour, and I got to know her on a much more personal level than I had before.

At the end of our conversation, we had come to an agreement that she was going to set a date, and clean out her house of everything she didn't need or wasn't using. She admitted during our conversation that she was a pack rat. She held onto everything, even if it had no sentimental value or was useless, and she did this "just in case" she might need it some day. So she did it – she set a date and cleared it all out, over the course of a weekend. She came in afterwards and told me she could actually feel a physical release in her body as she cleared everything out, and felt incredibly lighter. In the next two weeks that followed her "house cleaning," she lost about 20 pounds, and continued making progress after that as well.

Now, before I go on, I want to clarify something. I'm not saying that everyone that has to lose weight is a pack rat, like the woman in the story above. This was just the specific way that the inner and outer aspects of her life were reflective of each other. I worked with another woman who had a similar amount of weight to lose, but she wasn't a pack rat at all. In fact, she was just the opposite – she was excessively clean. She cleaned her house constantly, because she couldn't handle things being dirty. She didn't even like to sweat, because she felt it was gross. This woman was not willing to accept the dirty parts of life, or the "dirty" parts of herself, and because of this she stored them down deep, where they accumulated under the surface.

There is one more pattern that I recognized over the years that I would like to share with you – people that felt more of a sense of freedom and empowerment while following their program made progress toward their goals. On the other hand, those that felt more of a sense of restriction and struggle did not. Once I realized this, I stopped trying to get people to eliminate foods from their diet, or tell them that they couldn't do certain things. Instead, I used an inclusion approach. To give you an idea of what this means, here's an example:

> *I was once doing nutrition coaching with a man who wanted to lose weight, and when we first started working together I had him record some food logs for me, so I could get an idea of what his eating habits were. One of the things I noticed was that he drank two to*

three 16 oz. coffees every morning. Now, I ended up working with this man once a week for about half a year, but not once did I ever even mention the word "coffee." The first week I told him that I thought it would be beneficial if he could start drinking half his bodyweight in ounces of water every day. He said he could do this, so that became his weekly goal. The next week we added in some high water-content foods, and nothing else. In short, I kept having him add things into his diet that were beneficial, in small steps, and let the unhealthy foods drop off naturally. About two and a half months into working with each other, he told me that he was barely drinking any coffee at this point, which he thought was very interesting, because we had never talked about it. By the time we stopped working together, he had reached his weight loss goal, and had developed healthy eating habits that would help him maintain it – all with no restriction.

As you can probably imagine, all the studying I've done and the patterns I've recognized over almost two decades in the health industry have allowed me to help others much more effectively over the years. I would now like to tell you one more story. This story isn't about another pattern I recognized, or about another client having success. This story is about a personal experience I had – an experience that helped me to tie together all the past realizations I've made, and ultimately led me to write this book...

One night in early 2013, I was sitting in my front yard, getting ready to start my evening meditation. As I began to focus on my breathing, my mind started to slow down, and eventually it became very still. Suddenly, a memory popped into my head, as if to prevent me from going deeper into the stillness. It was a long lost memory of a question my father asked me when I was about 12 or 13 years old. The question was, "What happens when an unstoppable force meets with an immovable object?"

I got into a lot of trouble as a child, so whenever I was sent to my room, I would lie in bed and stare at the ceiling, trying to figure out what happens when a force that can't be stopped meets with an object that can't be moved. Eventually, I just figured it was an impossible situation, and stopped struggling with it.

I wasn't struggling with it now, though. No sooner had I remembered the question, than I had a vision of myself as a sperm cell, with a single positive charge, and I was surrounded by other sperm cells that were just like me. We were all flying in space, and I had no idea where we were going, but I knew we were heading somewhere. Eventually, we realized that we were all flying straight down toward a gigantic egg that had a huge negative charge. As my fellow sperm cells came into contact with the surface, their positive energies were discharged into the egg, causing electric shocks that jolted it. However, as more positive charges went into the egg, it brought the egg closer to a balance of positive and negative energy, and so the shocks became smaller and smaller, which moved the egg less and less. As fate would have it, I was special because I was able to pass through as the equilibrium of positive and negative energy was reached. Once I was inside, the egg repelled the other sperm, causing the now merged egg and sperm to become immovable – all the bumping had ceased. This immovability is where conception occurred. At that moment of conception, there immediately arose an unstoppable force, an explosion outward in all directions, that allowed this single cell to go through the process of transforming into a fully formed human being, made up of trillions and trillions of cells. The point in the middle – the point where the immovable egg met with the unstoppable force of expansion – is where my life began.

I found it to be the greatest of ironies that I was the answer I was looking for! I also thought it was very funny that I had always assumed the immovable object and unstoppable force were in opposition to each other, whereas in my vision they were complimentary and mutually creative. One couldn't exist without the other!

This was all very amazing to me, but it wasn't the end of my vision. Next, I saw a star in the sky, right before it was about to explode. This star had a dense metal core, with fire and light all around it. The core was so dense, and its gravitational force was so strong, that objects were flying into it from space. As these objects hit it, they caused tremors that slightly moved the surface. However, each object that hit it also caused its core to become more and more dense, and so it moved less and less with each collision. Eventually, its density and gravitational force were so strong that it had attracted all the objects it could from surrounding space, and there was nothing left to hit it. At this point the star reached critical mass. The light surrounding the core bent in on itself, and the entire star collapsed inward to the center, becoming an immovable object. It then immediately exploded outward, with unstoppable force, in all directions of the universe.

So now I had a sense that not only was I the answer, the answer was all around me – inside and out, from microcosm to macrocosm! There is nowhere I could look that did not contain the answer because all of existence is made of the exact same energy. I can't describe the feeling of awe this experience brought me, but I can tell you the most important thing I realized from it...

NOW is all that exists, and if we are going to live a healthy and fulfilling life, we can only do it NOW! The rest of this book is a guide for doing just this.

CHAPTER 1:

BUILDING THE FOUNDATION

IMMOVABLE HEART, UNSTOPPABLE MIND

This book is about becoming an exploding star of abundance, connection, growth, joy and freedom in our own lives. We do this by cultivating an immovable heart, so that we can be loving and compassionate, regardless of the circumstances around us. We also do this by cultivating an unstoppable mind, so that we can have the inner fortitude to think, speak and act from and for the highest good, and not be swayed to discontinue this journey or take a lower path, regardless of how enticing it may be to do so. When we become immovable in our hearts and unstoppable in our minds, we are able to experience extraordinary heights and cultivate remarkable things, without struggling to do so.

When we look at the most truly inspiring figures throughout history, they exemplified this. They were all immovable and unstoppable in some way. The reason they inspire us is because they show us more of ourselves than we are normally able to see. They show us our true power, the innate goodness that we possess, and the amazing things that we can do when we realize this. We have the ability to make an impact on this entire world – every single one of us.

My goal with this book is not to become a great inspirational figure that everyone follows. I don't believe that is what the world needs now. My goal is to bring clarity to the challenges we face in such a simple way, that we can all become inspirational figures together. It seems to me that the subject of health is the most logical choice for cultivating an immovable heart and unstoppable mind. It is the one all-encompassing subject that is relevant and important to all of us. It also doesn't create the division that emotionally charged subjects such as politics and religion can bring. The goal here is to focus on how we are connected. We can only have a big impact together, if we come together.

With this being said, let's start at the beginning...

A NEW APPROACH TO HEALTH

What is health?

It is such a simple question, but one that we rarely slow down to ask ourselves. Maybe it's so simple that we don't even think to ask the question. We sure seem to be surrounded by a lot of answers, however, when it comes to health. We can go online and find all kinds of descriptions – some say it is a state that is free of illness and injury, others say it is a state of complete harmony of body, mind and spirit, and so on. Likewise, in my career I've asked many people what they think health is, and the answers I get are varied – they are usually reflective of where they are weak. For example, most obese people tell me that being healthy means having a slender body. Most alcoholics tell me that being healthy means being free of their addiction, or having it under better control. Most diabetics tell me that being healthy means being free of their disease, and so on...

What I have found over the years is that there is a fundamental problem with our answers. The vast majority of them tend to focus on a certain "state" where everything is going great, and for a number of reasons, this causes us to approach "getting healthy" in a very ineffective way.

I am proposing a new model of health in this book – one that I believe gets to the true essence of what health really is, and which will help to release us from many of the challenges we've had up to this point.

Health is the *process* that characterizes how we live our life. This process is continually shaped and transformed through the overall content of our thoughts and feelings.

Health is the all-encompassing subject of life, because health *is* life! Everything we experience comes to us through our thoughts and feelings, so our health not only determines the conditions of our physical body, but also of our relationships, how we make our livelihood, and how we function in everyday life.

Life is always changing, so when we perceive our health to be a process, it helps us to align ourselves with life and to live it more fully. Then "being healthy" is no longer a concrete, desired state, but rather a process that cultivates a life of greater joy and fulfillment. Likewise, "being unhealthy" isn't a specific undesired state, such as being obese or in pain, but rather a way of living that cultivates more struggle, disempowerment, and suffering.

Looking at health in this more fluid way helps us to "flow" with life, so to speak, and enjoy the journey, because we aren't so attached to specific circumstances and labeling them as good or bad. We are able to see a bigger picture. When we view health as a specific state, however, we tend to narrow our vision and live our life in states. Then yesterday becomes a "good day" because I lost 2 pounds, but today was a "bad day" because I gained it back again. Fixating on states brings about those vicious cycles, those emotional ups and downs that are so painful to our experience.

Focusing on the process allows us to realize greater states than we ever would have if we were fixated on them. Focusing on states, on the other hand, puts us on a roller coaster of suffering, and keeps us stuck.

THE ROOTS OF IMBALANCE

What is the source of this problem? And what do we need to do in order to change this and really start living a healthy life?

Cultivating health, and ever-greater joy and fulfillment, is not something we have to learn how to do. It is our natural way of living. However, we create obstructions to this natural flow by clinging to the past, and longing for the future.

We cling to the past because we feel incomplete or inadequate in some way. We will look more into how and why we do this in the next chapter, but for now it is important that we understand that these attachments can never make us feel complete, at least not in the long run, and end up creating more problems than they are worth. The natural byproduct of never feeling the lasting happiness that we seek is that we long for a future where everything is better. I'll be happier when I lose this extra weight…my life will be great once I meet my soul mate…I'll be set for life once my career gets off the ground and I'm making a lot of money…

The past that we cling to, and the future that we long for, both reinforce one thing – they *necessarily* make "now" unfulfilling.

When we feel unfulfilled in this moment, we end up feeling bad about ourselves, and believing that we need to struggle, limit, and restrict ourselves on a "health program," in order to achieve a better state that will make us feel good again. It's an unconscious form of self-punishment, and it doesn't do anything to improve our lives.

All the suffering we create for ourselves arises due to our fixation on states, because this continually puts our attention on the past or the future. All

the solutions to this suffering naturally arise when we focus on the process, because this continually brings our attention back to the present moment.

Let's look at this in practical terms with the first thing we typically do when starting a new health program, or any other program for that matter – setting goals.

THE NATURE OF GOALS

Setting goals, and taking action with goals in mind, can be very effective in helping us to live a healthy life – if we take a *process-focused approach* to them. Most of us take a state-focused approach, however, which is why goal setting usually ends in frustration and disappointment.

With the typical state-focused approach, I'll set a goal to lose 40 lbs., I'll fixate on losing 40 lbs., I'll believe the thought of losing 40 lbs. is what excites me, and I won't be happy until I reach the goal. I'll struggle and restrict myself on a health program to try to get there.

> *My health program becomes a vehicle that is supposed to take me to a desired destination in the future.*

When we become process-focused, however, our approach completely changes, because instead of fixating on the future, we bring the goal into the present. Do this: Think of a goal – something you would really like to achieve. Do you have it in mind? Ok, now ask yourself – why is achieving this goal important to me? Now, take this answer, and ask again – why is *this* important? If we keep asking ourselves "why?" and move down the layers, we *always* come to an emotion – and it's always a positive one. I've never had someone move down the layers and say, "because it feels restricting, and that's why I want it!" It is natural that we want to feel more empowerment, more joy, more of a sense of freedom, more connection, more confidence, etc.

> *Any goal we set is merely a symbol that shows us the emotions we want to experience more of in our lives right now.*

When we realize this, we see how important it is to take action toward our goals in ways that cultivate these positive emotions. We set our goal, but then we let go of our attachment to its future attainment, and the happiness we imagine it will bring. Instead, we use it as a guide for how to approach a health program, and how to effectively use that program to help us start living our goal *right now*. Happiness becomes more and more a part of our present when we do this, rather than our future – and the more it does, the more we see our "goal" showing up in our lives, without the fixation on achieving it.

With a process-focused approach such as this, we are able to see how ridiculous it is to struggle and restrict ourselves on a health program in order to "get there." It doesn't make sense to take actions on a daily basis that are limiting and frustrating, and believe that we will find freedom and joy at the end of it. A pattern of struggle cultivates more struggle. A pattern of joy cultivates more joy.

> **When we focus on the process, our health program is no longer a *vehicle to something we don't have*, but rather becomes *an exercise in expanding what we do have!***

You'll notice throughout this book that we will not talk about reaching goals, hitting goals, accomplishing goals, achieving goals, or attaining goals. All of these imply that our goal is something we don't have now. Instead, we will talk about nurturing goals, cultivating goals, and allowing goals to blossom. These imply that we already have the goals inside us – they just need to be brought out.

This approach to setting and working with goals brings great freedom into our lives, because the more we practice this exercise in expanding what we already have, and make this moment the priority, the less powerful our obstacles become. Issues with confidence become less relevant because we are no longer trying to get something we don't have, and frustration becomes less frequent because we are less attached to our ideas of how our progress should be going. Challenges that previously seemed overwhelming begin to fall away of their own accord.

Then from the eyes of others, we seem to be achieving great things. From our own eyes, however, we see that there is nothing to achieve, nothing to attain. We are simply cultivating more of what we've always had, and these "achievements" are merely the natural byproduct of that cultivation.

CHANGING OUR LIVES...RIGHT NOW

Does this sound like a way that you would like to live? Are you ready to shift your focus and start living in this moment? I truly hope so, because the world needs you to be ready. Nobody ever lay on their deathbed and wished they had spent more of their life watching television, and the world doesn't need you to be just one more person that ends their days wishing they had lived them differently. The world needs you to be something different, to take a different journey, and I promise you that no matter who you are, no matter what the circumstances of your life look like, you are capable of taking this journey. I also promise you that it is worth it. Living a life that is full of convenience and entertainment but empty of fulfillment is no way to live. I am speaking from personal experience, because I have lived on both sides of it. I have spent years of my life in frustration and depression, covering up my issues with ice cream and chocolate, and spending hours a day in front of the television. I had no idea how miserable I had become until I shifted my focus and started to come out of it.

We are at a critical time on this planet, with a tremendous amount of conflict on many different levels. People are angry with the government, they feel overpowered by big banks, they are fearful of the impacts of global warming, and the list goes on and on. Yes, this entire world is in the pressure cooker – right now. This is a blessing though, because through the pain of this pressure, we have the ability to change our focus and become a diamond. There will always be an interplay of light and dark, up and down, hot and cold, and the immovable and unstoppable. This interplay can be a battle, or it can be transformed into a dance. The battle brings about the pressure, but the dance is what makes the diamond. The world needs you to start dancing, so that through your example it can begin to dance as well.

THE SIX ESSENTIAL PRACTICES OF HEALTH

The following chapters of this book will discuss the six essential practices for living a joyful and fulfilling life – a healthy life. These practices will help us to cultivate our immovable and unstoppable nature, they will help us to transform our inner battles into a dance, and ultimately they will help us to transform the world – first by transforming ourselves. These practices are simple, anyone can cultivate them, but that doesn't mean they are easy. We must have an open mind, and we must be willing to move away from the familiar, even if just a little bit at first, in order for the new to begin to shine.

These practices will be very different from the typical state-focused recommendations. They won't discuss specific foods we should eat, but rather more effective approaches to *how we go about* eating. They won't recommend specific exercises, but rather how to exercise in more empowering ways. Every one of them is familiar to all of us, but none of them is what we would typically consider a "health" practice. They *are* though – they are the most important, most essential health practices we can cultivate.

These practices all have one common purpose – they all direct us away from self-absorption, from fixating on the problems we have. When we stop fixating on our problems, when we stop giving them energy, they become weaker. Then we can stop hiding, we can stop beating ourselves up, and we can stop holding on to things we no longer need. Instead, we become a vessel that the flow of optimal health and fulfillment can easily flow through, and there is nothing more joyful than this.

CHAPTER 2:

THE ESSENTIAL PRACTICE OF GENEROSITY

In the movie *The Usual Suspects*, Kevin Spacey's character makes a very powerful statement. He says, "The greatest trick the devil ever pulled, was convincing the world he didn't exist."

In the world of health, this statement definitely applies. We usually think the devil is processed food, genetics, lack of time, lack of discipline, lack of quality guidance, office jobs that create sedentary lifestyles, or any one of a multitude of other things that we feel we have no control over. Meanwhile, the real devil is right in front of our faces the entire time, yet remains unseen.

The real "devil" of health is our pattern of holding onto the past.

Keep in mind, it is not the past events *themselves* that are the problem, it is *our pattern of holding onto them* that is the problem. This holding on gives us a rigid identity, so we become less creative and able to adapt, it creates attachments and expectations that dictate our emotional states, and it causes us to desire a better future. It is the root of our "health problems" in every area of life.

In recent years, many of us have started to see that clinging to the past is creating obstacles to our progress, and so we now have more of a desire to let go of it. The problem, however, is that because we have a state-focused approach, we seek to emotionally or mentally clear *specific events* from our past. We may be able to do this, but if we don't address the *underlying pattern of clinging*, we will just form new attachments, and the obstacles will persist.

DESCRIPTION OF GENEROSITY

Generosity is the process-focused approach to dealing with the pattern of holding onto the past. We will look at how generosity helps us to deal with these restrictive patterns shortly, but first let's look at what generosity actually is.

Generosity is a joyful separation, a joyful parting of ways that seeks nothing in return.

When we practice generosity, we are giving, offering, or extending with a sincere desire to be helpful. It is giving for the pure joy of giving, and for no other reason. Generosity does not occur when we are giving in a way that creates more struggle for ourselves, or when we give because we were taught that there is a certain way we should give, and we would feel guilty if we did otherwise. Any giving that is done with expectations for a desired outcome, returned favors, or because we feel that we need to meet the expectations of others, is not true generosity. Any giving that is done with a desire for recognition is also not true generosity. I remember seeing a "Seinfeld" television episode where the character, George, is in a shop, standing next to a tipping jar. He tries to wait until the owner is looking before he puts his money in the jar, so that the owner will recognize his generosity. Although the story was funny, this is not generosity!

Some of us give so much that it depletes us, and is no longer joyful. When we give in this way, it's usually because we have difficulty setting boundaries, or want others to accept us and view us favorably. This is not generosity. True generosity is always joyful, and we are always energized and invigorated when we give in a generous way.

It is important that we understand these distinctions between giving purely and giving with a desire for some type of return, because unless we are practicing true generosity, our giving will not have the powerful impact on our lives that it otherwise could.

THE DIFFICULTY IN LETTING GO

I can remember many times in my life where I felt that I needed to let go of painful experiences from the past that were holding me back, but I didn't know how. It felt scary and painful to let them go, even though I knew my life would improve if I did. There seemed to be some type of inner resistance, as if releasing these experiences would be a movement into the unknown… the unfamiliar…the unsafe.

If this sounds like something you can relate to, you're not alone. It is very common for us to feel this way, and it doesn't mean there's something wrong with us. The reason we hold onto the past is because we feel inadequate, and the reason we feel inadequate is because in the beginning of life we *are*, in a sense, inadequate!

A natural part of the human experience is that we are helpless when we are born into this world. We are entirely dependent on our guardians to take care of us. At some point when we are babies, we realize our inadequacy and start trying to manipulate our environment to gain more power. We test the limits with our parents, other adults and children around us, and we focus on what we can get, what we can possess, what we can hold onto.

> *Grasping for what we can get, for what is "mine,"*
> *becomes one of our dominant childhood patterns.*

Sir Isaac Newton said that an object in motion will continue to stay in motion, unless acted upon by an outside force. This applies not only to objects, but to our habit patterns as well. Our pattern of focusing on what we can get will stay with us the rest of our lives, unless we consciously change the pattern. In smaller villages and communities throughout history, the elders knew this, and so they would apply an "outside force" in the form of rites of passages and initiations, when a child was becoming an adult. They realized that if adults continued the typical childhood pattern of focusing on "what can I get?" it would not serve the community well. So they would create initiations that were intense and dramatic enough to completely change this pattern. Afterwards, the new initiate would no longer be focused on what they can get, but rather on what they can give, and on how they can be of value and service to the community.

In modern-day society, not only do we no longer have rites of passage that will change this pattern in our young adults, we actually *strengthen* the childhood pattern. Adults are bombarded by thousands of stimuli everyday that reinforce convenience, entertainment, and possession. When we watch commercials or look on the covers of any of our popular magazines, we only see messages about what we can get. We don't see messages like "5 ways to bring more abundance into the lives of your loved ones!" Instead we see "5 easy tips for making more money!"

Is it any surprise that the majority of our marriages end in divorce? When we have two adults that come together, and through years of conditioning are focused on what they can get out of the relationship, rather than what they can give to it, isn't that a recipe for dysfunction? How about in the workplace? We have bosses that are trying to get as much as they can out of their employees, and employees that are doing just enough to fill the requirements that are needed to receive a paycheck. Is it any wonder that most people don't like their jobs?

We search in the Self Help sections of bookstores, looking for ways to improve our lives, and we practice the Law of Attraction to try to manifest more of what we want, but very few of us can actually say that this approach has radically transformed our lives. How could it? We put our energy into practicing the Law of Attraction without putting nearly as much energy into the equally important and powerful Law of Repulsion (Generosity). We're like a rocket ship on the ground that is grasping for objects in space, to try to pull ourselves up to the moon. We'll never leave the ground with this pattern of grasping. In order to leave the ground, we must release, we must let go – we must cultivate the pattern of giving.

GENEROSITY AND HEALTH

We all know that generosity is a very positive trait, but rarely do we think of it in regards to our health. However, it has a very important and necessary function. As we discussed earlier, the act of "letting go" of our attachments is oftentimes scary and/or painful, because it moves us into the unknown and unfamiliar, and challenges our feelings of safety and security. Our inability to "let go" keeps obstructions alive, and keeps us where we are – stuck.

Before I realized the power of generosity, I spent years trying to remove my mental and emotional hang-ups. Not only was this oftentimes painful and frustrating, I also began to realize there was a big dilemma that was created with this approach. What I found was that the very act of mentally or emotionally "clearing" attachments from the past was putting my attention on them, and this kept them alive. So even if I cleared a specific attachment, the overall concept of "I have attachments that need to be cleared" was being strengthened, and so in order to continue this pattern of clinging, other attachments would form to take the cleared one's place. For years I asked myself "Is there a way to release the past without putting my attention on it, which is keeping the pattern of clinging alive?"

The answer is yes – generosity is the way to do this.

Cultivating the practice of generosity helps us to let go of obstructions without putting our attention on them. It is able to do this because when we develop the habit of giving purely, *we re-pattern our minds to associate release with joy, rather than with pain.*

The more we make generosity a regular practice in our daily lives, the more we re-pattern our minds to enjoy letting go, rather than to fear it. In my own life, I've noticed that attachments begin to fall away with no effort, like ripe apples falling from a tree, and it happens whenever I'm not expecting it. I may be out for a walk, or cooking, and all of the sudden I'll have a flutter of thoughts move through my mind. These thoughts may have disturbed me quite a bit in the past, but now it's as if they're made of soap bubbles and are harmless, and I'll just observe them moving by like I'm watching a movie of someone else's life.

I know this may sound funny, but not only does releasing the past not have to be painful, it can at times even be orgasmic. The feeling of lightness and vitality we can experience when we no longer burden ourselves with heavy baggage is truly amazing. I can honestly say that in my own life, cultivating the practice of generosity has brought me more of a sense of freedom and empowerment than I ever could have imagined.

PRACTICAL APPLICATION

For most of my life, generosity was not a focus for me because I didn't have a lot of money. I told myself that I would be more generous in the future, when I had the ability to do so. This approach was effective at keeping me feeling a sense of lack in my present circumstances, while abundance was continually pushed to the future. Eventually, I was fortunate enough to realize that our ability to practice generosity has nothing to do with how much money or physical possessions we can give away. Generosity does not have to be a future thing; everyone has the ability to be generous right now, no matter what one's present circumstances are. It is only when we realize this and then practice it, that we are truly able to live an abundant life.

Here are some practical tips for getting started on the practice of generosity:

1. Make Your Goal Bigger Than Yourself

What is your health goal? That's the first question. Now, here's the second: How are you going to give more, be more helpful, and bring more value to others, through the cultivation of your goal?

Most of us are quick to ask the first question, but rarely do we ask the second. However, it is equally important. When our goals only concern ourselves, they are selfish goals. When we expand them to be of benefit to others in some way, they are unselfish goals. Unselfish goals are much more powerful than selfish goals, because they have the power of generosity behind them, and they inspire us to be and do more than we normally would.

Tell a woman there is a $20,000 prize for her, but she has to cross a narrow, rickety bridge that spans a deep canyon, and enter a burning house to get it, and she'll probably have doubts about her ability to do it, or just say the money isn't worth the risk of falling off the bridge or being burned alive. There are many factors that could come into her mind that would prevent her from moving forward. However, put her baby in the house and she will run across that bridge and into the house like a bat out of hell, without giving it a second thought. This woman is immovable in her love for her baby, and her determination makes her unstoppable in the face of danger.

When our goals are unselfish and generous enough, we *always* become immovable and unstoppable.

In my experience as a personal trainer, the people who were successful were always people who had expanded their goals to include others. A person could be struggling for months or years to get motivated enough to lose weight, then they join a sports team and all of a sudden motivation is no longer an issue, and the weight is flying off. They couldn't find the motivation for themselves, but there was no way they were going to be the weak link that brought the rest of the team down. Their desire to give, to contribute to the team, made them stronger. With other people, the struggle would end when they started to see their children adopting an unhealthy lifestyle, and they suddenly had a desire to be a role model for them. Still others developed the desire to work in the health and fitness industry themselves, so they could help others who were dealing with the same struggles that they were dealing with. This is why many health professionals are their own first success story.

Take the time to really look at your goal, and expand it to include others in a way that gets you emotionally charged up. The challenge is not a lack of discipline or motivation; the challenge is to find a greater purpose for your goal that naturally brings a sense of determination.

2. Determine Your "Goal Emotions," And Then Give Them Away.

In the previous chapter, we discussed how goals are really just symbols for what we want to feel more of in our lives right now. When we move down the layers of our goals, by continually asking ourselves why it is important, we eventually come to our "goal emotions." Below is an example of how this works, from my own life.

MY GOAL: To write a book

Q: Why is this important to me?

A: Because I have something valuable to share that will bring clarity to what is really holding us back from living a life of optimal health, as well as what it really takes to release this and start living it.

Q: And why is *this* important to me?

A: Because by bringing clarity to these things, I can help others to change their lives.

Q: And why is *this* important to me?

A: Because I feel joyful in the thought of helping others, and I feel empowered by the thought that I can have an impact, as well as a sense of freedom because I am doing something that I truly have a passion for.

GOAL EMOTIONS: Joy, Empowerment, Freedom

Now, once I have these goal emotions, I let go of my attachment to completing the book, and I start to focus on giving my goal emotions away in everything I do. What this means is that throughout my day, regardless of what I'm doing, I find ways to help others feel more joy, empowerment and freedom. If I'm at the grocery store, I find ways to compliment people. If I'm talking with a friend, I see them as strong and powerful, so they can begin to see themselves that way also. If I'm writing, I set the intention to write in a way that will bring my goal emotions to whomever is reading my words.

When I give away my goal emotions in my daily activities, it makes whatever I'm doing more powerful, because it infuses it with a greater purpose than just my own self-interests.

3. Give Away 10% Of Your Income

Most of us have had such a strong focus on what we can grab hold of, that making a dramatic shift to focusing predominantly on what we can give is unrealistic. These shifts are usually more effective if we take them in bite-size pieces. For this reason, I recommend that we begin by giving 10% of our income.

Now, before we go on, I want to clarify what I mean by income. Income is *not* just money. Income is whatever is *coming in* to our experience. So whatever we are experiencing, whether eating, talking, running errands – whatever it is, we should find creative ways to give during 10% of the time that we are experiencing it. As this practice becomes more and more familiar, we naturally begin to give more and more over time. For example, when I sit down to eat a meal, I like to dedicate the benefit I will get from the meal to all beings. Then I start eating with this intention in mind. Before I exercise, I set the intention to use any strength I will get from it to help others become stronger, then I start exercising with this intention in mind. When I get ready to wash the dishes, I set the intention to cleanse myself of anything that is preventing me from seeing my innate goodness through the act of washing the dishes, so that I can help others to do so as well. Then I start washing the dishes with this intention in mind. When I'm driving, I take some time to give thanks and appreciation to the trees that I see on the way.

These are just a few examples of little things we can do to practice generosity. The more we set the intention to give 10% during our daily experiences, the more we will see creative ways to practice generosity that we didn't see before.

THE POWER OF GENEROSITY

Viktor Frankl was a survivor of the Nazi concentration camps who wrote a book called *Man's Search For Meaning*. In his book, he describes the incredible pain and suffering that he and his fellow prisoners went through – pain, he says, that the typical person can't even begin to imagine. Everything they had was stripped from them, they were made to work under extreme and cruel conditions, and they were so starved that they practically became walking skeletons.

One of the interesting things he observed while in the camps was the very obvious sign of when a prisoner lost hope. This occurred when the prisoner no longer felt any meaning or purpose for his or her life, when there was nothing left to live for. They were typically dead within 48 hours.

Viktor Frankl realized that if he was going to keep any measure of hope, he needed to find some kind of purpose for his suffering. So he started to imagine himself lecturing to audiences about what they were going through in the camps, in order to help others to be aware of it and prevent the same thing from happening again in the future.

This vision was an act of generosity, and it not only gave meaning to the pain he was going through, it also made his survival bigger than just his own self-interests. He was living for much more than himself. In fact, this act of generosity was so powerful that it made him immovable and unstoppable. He realized that no matter what the Nazis did to him, the one thing they had no control over was how he would choose to respond to it. He called this *the last human freedom*, and when he realized this freedom, he responded with an immovable love, regardless of what others did to him, and he became unstoppable in his willingness to help others in any way he could.

Viktor Frankl not only survived the holocaust and lived out his vision, he became an inspiration to millions all over the world, and was a big influence on many leaders in self-help and personal development, as well as in the field of psychology.

REGAINING OUR POWER

Although we may not have gone through the types of experiences that Viktor Frankl did, we all have our own "inner-holocaust" going on right now. The guards of our inner-holocaust are the obstructions we create by holding onto the past, and the prisoners are the happiness, joy, and freedom that we all have, but are hidden, restricted, starved, and struggling to get out. The obstructions prevent the natural flow of optimal health, they get us to doubt our ability to cultivate our goals, and they convince us that our health is not in our control. We cannot gain power over our obstructions by focusing on them. That will only have the opposite affect – it will make them stronger. We can only gain power over them by finding a purpose for cultivating our health that is greater than ourselves. We can only gain power over them by practicing generosity.

CHAPTER 3:

THE ESSENTIAL PRACTICE OF INTEGRITY

The power of generosity is truly able to start having a big impact in our life when we begin to cultivate the second essential practice of optimal health – the practice of integrity.

Whereas generosity helps us to release obstructions with more joy, integrity helps us to not create new obstructions to begin with.

When we live a life of integrity, we no longer take actions that create small, or large, amounts of baggage that accumulate and turn into overwhelming obstacles later on. We can stand behind our behavior with confidence, because we are seeking to act in ways that bring the highest good for all involved. We no longer lie to make our circumstances more comfortable, or gossip in order to vent or create alliances. So, we no longer create the obstructions that arise when we have something to hide. Likewise, by conducting ourselves with a spirit of compassion and helpfulness, we no longer create the obstructions that arise when we act in ways that bring regret, remorse, or feelings of guilt. Conducting ourselves in a way that prevents this type of baggage from being created has an enormous impact on the sense of freedom and inner security we can feel in our lives. On top of this, it is only through the practice of integrity that we are able to build a strong foundation for our relationships – both with others and with ourselves.

DESCRIPTION OF INTEGRITY

Integrity is the companion of generosity, and when we are truly practicing one, we are also practicing the other. Integrity is the coming together that complements generosity's moving apart. When we give with no expectation of a return, this is generosity. The connection we feel through our generosity is integrity.

> **Integrity is a unification, a connecting, a coming together, that brings about inner fortitude and strength.**

Conducting ourselves with integrity means we are being positive in thought and feeling. This means we are honest *and* compassionate, because honesty brings about inner fortitude of thought, word and action, and compassion brings about inner fortitude of feeling. We need them both to be in integrity. When we act with integrity, we are acting with a desire to be helpful, rather than harmful or hurtful. For many years of my life, I thought I was a person of integrity because I was very honest in what I said to people. However, during those times when I was being "brutally honest" or using the so-called "truth" to build my own case while breaking another's down, I was not acting with integrity.

> *Integrity goes right out the window when "being right" is more important than connecting.*

Integrity always strengthens and connects; a lack of integrity always weakens and separates. This is why something that is becoming weakened and experiencing separation is *dis-integrating.*

Personal integrity is very much the same as the structural integrity that is needed when an object, such as a bridge, is being constructed. A bridge needs to be built with strong, sturdy materials, but these materials must also be configured in such a way that provides optimal stability. Only when it has the right materials *and* the right configuration can cars drive over it, and storms move through it, without it being adversely affected.

Earlier in this book we discussed our new paradigm for health; one that views health as a process – a process that is continually shaped and transformed through the overall content of our thoughts and feelings Thoughts and feelings are the materials and configurations that make up the realm of integrity, and they will be the focus of this chapter.

OBSTACLES TO INTEGRITY

In order to practice integrity, we must give attention to both our thoughts *and* our feelings. This means we are conscious of what we are thinking, saying and doing, and at the same time sensitive to what we are feeling. The more we do this, the more harmonious our life will be. On the other hand, when we give more attention to one at the expense of the other, we experience disharmony and suffering. All the obstacles to integrity arise because of this imbalance of attention between our thoughts and feelings.

In looking at the ways we live in the world, there are three general types of interactions we can have, with others and ourselves, as shown below:

1. FEELINGS EMPHASIZED OVER THOUGHTS	=	**AGGRESSION**
2. THOUGHTS EMPHASIZED OVER FEELINGS	=	**AVOIDANCE**
3. ATTENTIVE TO BOTH THOUGHTS AND FEELINGS	=	**INTEGRITY**

Integrity is the only type of interaction we can have that brings lasting connection and harmony. The other two bring short-term comfort, but long-term dysfunction and suffering. Let's now take a look at these other two types of interactions, these obstacles to integrity, so that we can better see the consequences of *not* living with integrity, and how this influences the way we cultivate our health.

AGGRESSION:

Aggression is a dysfunctional outward movement of energy. It naturally arises when we've been holding things in through avoidance, and have an excessive build-up of energy that needs to be released. This build-up of energy creates a pressure inside us, and this pressure causes us to put more of our attention on what we're feeling, and less of it on what we're thinking, saying and doing.

This is why we can feel exhilarated in the moment of aggression, but then regret what we said or did afterwards – we are less focused on our thoughts, words and actions because our feelings are running the show.

Aggression arises in disagreeable circumstances where our built-up energy influences us to handle the situation by attacking or confronting, so that we can regain a sense of power and feel good again. When this involves others, we see their behavior as threatening to our wellbeing, so our communication is meant to be disruptive, to break the other down, and to show them that their behavior is creating problems.

Aggression can range from physical or emotional violence to subtle manipulations that are meant to "fix" things (or show how they're broken). In the short-term, aggression brings a sense of power because we are controlling, manipulating or dominating. However, the natural consequence of excessively releasing this energy is that we feel empty and remorseful afterward. With this emptiness, we naturally move into avoidance.

AVOIDANCE:
Avoidance is a dysfunctional inward movement of energy. It naturally arises after we've acted with aggression, and caused a separation that makes us feel empty and hollow inside. Our

energy becomes depleted when we feel empty, and this causes us to put less of our attention on what we're feeling, and more of it on what we're thinking, saying and doing.

> *This is why avoiding unpleasant circumstances can bring a sense of relief in the moment, but can bring feelings of anger or resentment later on – we are more concerned with keeping the peace with our thoughts, words and actions, and less focused on the tension that builds up from not expressing how we really feel.*

Avoidance arises in disagreeable circumstances where our depleted energy influences us to handle the situation by retreating or hiding, and trying to keep the peace, so that we don't cause conflict. When this involves others, we see ourselves as threatening to their wellbeing, so our communication is meant to keep things settled and calm, and to make them believe that everything is fine.

Avoidance can range from physical or emotional betrayal to the little white lies we tell (or truths we omit) in order to keep our circumstances comfortable. In the short-term, avoidance brings peace of mind because conflict has been prevented. However, the natural consequence of painting a pretty picture on the outside is that we hold in what we really feel on the inside.

When the pressure of holding in our emotions becomes great enough, we naturally move into aggression.

VICIOUS CYCLES

As you can tell from the descriptions above, aggression moves into avoidance and avoidance moves into aggression. In fact, all the vicious cycles of suffering that we experience are, in some form or another, movements back and forth between aggression and avoidance. I get upset with your behavior, and I lash out at you in anger. Later on, when I calm down, I realize I may have gotten carried away with my feelings, and said things that I wish I hadn't. This makes me feel regretful about my actions, and feel the need to make up for it. So now, when you behave in ways that upset me, I'm not as quick to address it. Everything seems to be going fine for a while, but meanwhile I'm holding it in, and holding it in, and holding it in…until I can't hold it in anymore. Then the whole cycle starts over again.

Of course, this is a simplified version of the cycle, because it involves only you and me. In most cases, however, it involves many people and circumstances. I may have been holding things in for a while, in many different areas of my life, and you may happen to be the person that triggers me the most – or you may just be in the wrong place at the wrong time when

I've reached the breaking point, and my build-up of energy tips over into aggression.

It's pretty easy to see how these vicious cycles can have a destructive impact on our relationships with others, but do they also apply to our relationship with ourselves?

Absolutely. Take the following scenario:

> *Jane is overweight, and has been for years. In the morning she wakes up, looks in the mirror, and with a disgusted look on her face she thinks to herself, "I am so fat." This thought produces a negative feeling, which brings her down and makes her feel bad about herself. However, she continues to do this every morning. Why?*

This type of scenario is extremely common, and even if our own specific circumstances are different from Jane's, I think we can all relate in some way to what it feels like when we use negative self-talk. Jane's habit of putting herself down every morning is an act of avoidance. She is giving more attention to the thoughts she is having than to the way these thoughts make her feel. If she was giving more attention to her feelings, she may say...

"You know what? Giving myself these negative messages doesn't feel good, and it doesn't do anything positive for me. I don't want to live my life feeling like this anymore, so I'm going to start making an effort to be more positive and loving with myself."

This would be a movement toward integrity. However, it can be a hard movement for Jane to make, because the negative self-talk has become such a strong habit for her. It is familiar, it is what she is used to, it is within her "comfort zone." It takes energy to move into the unfamiliar and change a habit, even if it's one that makes us feel bad. It is much easier to just stay on autopilot, to keep things the way they are, to not "make waves" in the normal routine. It's easier to stay in avoidance.

Jane doesn't put energy and attention into changing this dysfunctional pattern, so the negative feelings build up inside her. And the story continues...

After thinking "I am so fat" and getting herself into a negative emotional state, Jane heads to work. While driving, she notices someone riding a bicycle, and thinks, "I am too heavy to ever do anything like that." When she gets to work, she talks with her co-worker about how hard it is to stay on a diet, because she has no discipline. When she goes to the restroom, she repeats the morning mirror routine...

As we noticed earlier through Sir Isaac Newton – an object in motion will continue to stay in motion, unless acted upon by an outside force. Jane continues to think, say and do things that accumulate negative feelings, because she hasn't put energy into an "outside force" that would change this pattern...

Eventually, Jane gets home from work. Soon after walking in the door, she finds herself in front of the freezer, staring at a pint of ice cream. Her mind says, "I shouldn't eat this, because I'm trying to lose weight." However, she really feels like having it – and this time her feelings overpower her thoughts. She grabs the pint, and closes the freezer door...

We can only inhale for so long – eventually we must exhale. We can only hold in our feelings for so long – eventually we must release them. In this example, Jane is releasing them by eating ice cream. This is an act of aggression. She has switched her focus, and is now giving more attention to her feelings, and less attention to her thoughts about whether or not it is a good idea to indulge in her cravings. Eating the ice cream will feel good in the moment, but eventually she will feel guilty and weak for "caving in," and wish she hadn't done it. This will cause Jane to beat herself up, which further strengthens her pattern of avoidance, and keeps the cycle going.

It's easy to look at these two situations...

1. Negative self-talk (thoughts overpower feelings)
2. Eating ice cream (feelings overpower thoughts)

...and think they are two separate events. They are not. They are actually two aspects of one cyclical event that never ends – until we do something about it. It's only the pause in between each aspect that gives us the perception that they are separate, and not connected to each other. If you and I were watching two kids playing on a seesaw for half an hour, it would be easy for us to see that each time one of them goes up it causes the other to go down, and vice versa. Because we can see this connection between them, we view the entire scenario as one event, not as a separate event with each up-and-down. Even if one of the kids got off to tie his shoe, then got right back on, we wouldn't say the kids played on the seesaw on two separate occasions – we would still see it as the same event. *Our vicious cycles are the same way, only with a greater pause in between each up and down.*

In the same way that a seesaw can't function if there isn't a person on each end, our vicious cycles can't exist if we don't feed them and make them stronger with our avoidance and aggression.

Regardless of the simplicity or complexity of our vicious cycles, they are very much living entities – and these living entities need to receive food and release waste in order to survive, just like any other living entity. Avoidance is the food, and aggression is the waste, that gives life to our vicious cycles.

INTEGRITY AND HEALTH

The practice of integrity helps us to diminish the power of this cycle, and the impact that it has on our life, because we are no longer making it stronger by feeding it or allowing it to release its waste. The desire to take up this practice, by cultivating honesty *and* compassion, arises when we realize that we are creating our own vicious cycle of suffering by looking for short-term comfort, and we no longer have a desire to do this anymore. When we really begin to see that everything we experience in this physical existence comes to us through our thoughts and feelings, we realize that the amount of care and attention we give to them has a huge impact on how we perceive the world around us.

We don't see the world as it is – we see it as *we* are!

The world is mirroring us back to ourselves, because everything we experience comes to us through the filter of our own minds. This is why you and I can view the exact same event and have completely different ideas about what happened. For example, if we take a walk in the park together, your pattern of connecting may cause you to appreciate the beauty of the flowers, the sunlight coming through the trees, the smell of cut grass, and the fresh air. On the other hand, my pattern of trying to solve problems may cause me to notice that there is some litter on the ground, and start complaining because there are not enough trashcans to support the size of the park. We are in the same place, but in two different worlds.

> **If I'm focused on problems, I'll see more and more problems in the world. If I have a tendency toward anger, I'll find things to be angry about. If I'm focused on connecting, I will have experiences that help me feel closer and more intimate with others.**

This is an easy concept to understand, but not so easy to put into practice, especially when dealing with other people. Sometimes it can be extremely difficult to see how something unpleasant that we are experiencing is a reflection of us. However, when we do make the effort to see the connection, we are acting with integrity, and it can be rewarding in ways we would never expect. Here are the two fundamental steps for getting started in the practice of integrity.

1. USE SELF-REFLECTION TO FIND THE CONNECTION

When we begin to see that we have been triggered, meaning that someone or something has pushed our buttons and our emotional state is disturbed, a beneficial way to deal with this uprising of emotional energy is to use it for self-reflection. By practicing self-reflection before the emotional build-up becomes too big, we have the ability to decrease our aggressive tendencies, because we are able to start seeing connections where we previously couldn't. It's easy to point the finger at someone else when we don't see their connection with us. When we do, however, our behavior can change drastically.

> *I once worked with a man who I perceived to be a terrible listener. This was very frustrating for me, because I couldn't see the connection between us – I felt I was a good listener. However, I knew that if this was frustrating for me, it must be telling me something about myself that*

I wasn't seeing. There had to be a connection somewhere. So I started to really look at my life, and what I found was that although I listened well when it came to communicating with most people, I didn't listen well in other areas of my life. The biggest area was eating. I would usually read or watch TV when I was eating, which means I wasn't sensitive to the signals my body was sending me about the food I was eating, or the way I was eating it. So I stopped distracting myself and started to pay attention to my food. What happened was amazing. Over the course of a few months, my cravings for emotional "cover up" foods began to greatly diminish, my digestion improved tremendously, I started to have strong desires for vegetables and salads (which never appealed to me before), and I stopped taking naps regularly in the middle of the day because I had much more energy. I was less and less bothered by my co-worker, because I could see the gift he was giving me through this experience, and it wasn't long before he got a new job and left anyway.

Eating cleaner food, in a more effective way, helped me to gain greater clarity than I ever had before. I was able to organize a lot of the knowledge about health that I had had in my head, and see a way that I could communicate it that would make sense. If I had taken the easy, more comfortable route, and just seen my co-worker as the source of my frustration, rather than taking responsibility for my own frustration and looking deeper into myself to find the connection with him, it is very likely that no growth would have come from this experience.

Deciding to practice integrity means we are deciding to take responsibility for our life, and our emotional state – even when it isn't pleasurable to do so. It's much easier to see someone else as the reason we are upset, rather than to look deep inside to find the connection – to see what they are showing us about ourselves. However, unless we are willing to start making efforts to do this, even in small steps at first, we will never know true freedom, and we will never be truly empowered. We will be like a bridge that collapses whenever a storm comes its way.

2. RE-SENSITIZE YOURSELF

Have you ever had an angry outburst that seemed to come out of nowhere? As if there was a ton of built-up energy, but you weren't aware of it until it came out?

I think we can all admit that we've experienced this to some extent in our lives. We live in a very thinking-based society, with all sorts of stimulation and distraction for our minds, and because of this we have become very desensitized to our bodies. This desensitization makes it very difficult for us to feel the beginning stages of emotional build-up, and oftentimes we don't become aware of it until it comes out. We must find a way to rebalance this societal emphasis on the mind, if we want to live a life of greater harmony. Re-sensitizing ourselves is the way to restore this balance.

Whereas self-reflection helps us to deal with emotional energy more effectively, so that we don't move so quickly into aggression, re-sensitizing ourselves helps us to be more aware of when the build-up of energy begins to occur, so that we don't move so deeply into avoidance.

Re-sensitizing ourselves helps us in more ways than just preventing angry outbursts. I recently attended a lecture by an expert in health and electromagnetic technologies. Before the lecture began, I overheard a woman talking with some of her friends. She was explaining how excited she was because she was *finally* going to be able to find out what she should be eating. I could relate to this woman; I've had many times in my life where I looked to a person, or a book, or something else to tell me the solution to my problems, and as a health professional, I've also worked with a lot of people that came to me for health guidance with the same mindset.

The comforts and convenience of modern day life have caused many of us to become so desensitized and out of touch with our bodies that we believe others know what is best for us more so than we do ourselves. We give more credibility to popular opinion, or to someone else's title, than we do to signals we get from our own bodies.

I remember having a conversation with someone who came to see me because she wanted to lose a significant amount of weight. She told me that when she was younger she was very thin and energetic. I asked if she ate differently at that time than she does now. She said yes – she ate a lot of fatty foods. I then asked her what happened, and she told me that she eventually learned that fatty foods were bad, so she stopped eating them. She then began to gain weight and become more lethargic over the years. By the time I spoke with her, which was many years and many pounds later, she had never thought to question what she learned, to see if maybe it wasn't accurate in her case. She was in a pattern of avoidance, because she gave more value to the information she had gathered with her mind than she did to the feelings she was experiencing in her body. The first thing I did with her was to get her to start eating more fatty foods, and she immediately started losing weight and feeling better.

The above case is not uncommon. I've worked with *many* people over the years who have had similar challenges. It is admittedly much easier to just believe that the experts can tell us the answers than it is to practice becoming sensitive to our bodies so that we can find the answers for ourselves. However, unless we begin to practice cultivating this sensitivity, we aren't really able to experience the vitality and joy that come from being truly empowered in our health.

This is not to say that it is a problem to get advice from the "experts." The problem arises when we take the advice as truth before we even try it, or when we do try it and our bodies tell us something different, but we continue to believe it anyway. When we receive guidance with an open mind, and use it with a spirit of exploration, then we have the ability to move further into self-discovery and personal growth.

PRACTICAL APPLICATION

Be persistent – start with the little things. In most cases, the desire for instant gratification brings short-term pleasure, but does very little to increase the amount of happiness and fulfillment that we experience in the long run. The practical exercises of self-reflection and re-sensitization aren't exciting, and they don't usually bring the quick results that appeal to our desires for instant gratification (in fact, nothing in this book really does that). They do, however, help us to feel more balanced and fulfilled in the long run, with persistent practice.

The key to effectively implementing these practices is not to focus on being at a specific *state* of proficiency all the time, but rather to focus on the *process*.

We are not looking to be perfect, we are just looking to make progress.

In my own life, I have plenty of room for improvement when it comes to integrity. I move into aggression and avoidance at times, just like others do. However, by making a conscientious effort to improve on my integrity, what I've found is that I move into aggression and avoidance much less frequently than I used to. Things that I used to get very angry about a few years ago, now have significantly less impact on me. Situations that I would get emotionally disturbed about for days, weeks, or even months, now get me disturbed for minutes. This is a long maturation – a blossoming that can't be forced or hurried. Beating ourselves up for not being perfect is counterproductive, and only serves to keep us entrenched in our vicious cycle of suffering that much longer. It's important that we accept where we are, know that we are going to falter at times, and understand that if we stay persistent with the practice, we will falter less frequently and less intensely over time.

Taking up the practical steps that cultivate integrity is usually most effective when we start with the little things that aren't too challenging. For example, self-reflection may be very difficult at first with things that really trigger us and seem to be the complete opposite of us, but easier with things that are only slightly unpleasant. Self-reflection takes creativity, and the more we self-reflect and build our "creative muscles," by finding the connections with our smaller challenges, the easier it will become to see the connection with the more challenging circumstances in our lives. Likewise, re-sensitizing ourselves and becoming in-tune with our bodies goes against the grain of our normal conditioning, so it's beneficial to take it in bite-sized pieces. For example, it may be difficult to feel into the body during a conversation, but easy to do so while eating, or brushing the teeth, or going to the bathroom. Similarly, it may be difficult to feel into the body while sitting at a computer, but easy to do so while taking a walk or exercising. When we develop the pattern of becoming more sensitive to the body during these easier activities, the more difficult ones eventually won't be so difficult.

FREEING A NATION WITH INTEGRITY

As we can see, integrity shapes every area of our lives. It shows us the inner workings of our relationships with others, and ourselves, and what we can do to improve them. It shows us that the way we deal with energy influences whether we feel empowered or disempowered, how we interact with the world, and how we perceive the circumstances we find ourselves in. It shows us that a health recommendation can set one person free while enslaving another, because it isn't just the recommendation itself, it's also our approach to taking it that determines its effectiveness.

One of the greatest examples of integrity that I've come across in modern times is Nelson Mandela. Although serving a life-sentence for anti-apartheid activism, he never stopped working for the freedom of his people in South Africa. He became inspired by a poem written by William Ernest Henley, called *Invictus*, and would recite it to the other prisoners. Here is that poem:

INVICTUS

Out of the night that covers me,
Black as the pit from pole to pole,
I thank whatever gods may be
For my unconquerable soul.
In the fell clutch of circumstance
I have not winced nor cried aloud.
Under the bludgeonings of chance
My head is bloody, but unbowed.
Beyond this place of wrath and tears
Looms but the horror of the shade,
And yet the menace of the years
Finds, and shall find me, unafraid.
It matters not how strait the gate,
How charged with punishment the scroll,
I am the master of my fate.
I am the captain of my soul.

Very similarly to Viktor Frankl, who we read about in the last chapter, it seems that Nelson Mandela found a place of empowerment and freedom within himself that no one could ever take away. He became the "master of his fate" and the "captain of his soul," by taking responsibility for his life and living with integrity.

Living with integrity meant taking the high road. Rather than seeking retribution for the hardships he went through, and the hardships of his people, he sought to break the cycle of suffering altogether, not only for his people, but for *all* of South Africa, and for future generations of blacks *and* whites. He realized that if the blacks eventually took power and violently punished and oppressed the whites, his people would become what they had always despised, and the cycle of suffering and violence would continue. This would not bring about peace and freedom in South Africa.

So what did he do?

Something astonishing. When he was eventually released, after spending 27 years in prison, he forgave those who oppressed and imprisoned him, and worked closely with them in efforts to abolish apartheid, promote equality, and peacefully bring about racial reconciliation. He became the first black President of South Africa, won the Nobel Peace Prize, and became known by many as "the father of the nation."

Nelson Mandela was not completely free of anger. By his own admission, there was a part of him that *did* want to punish his oppressors. However, he wanted freedom and peace even more, and what made him great was that he chose to conduct himself with this greater vision in mind – with integrity – rather than be lured by the exhilarating temptation of getting payback. He became immovable in his compassion, regardless of the hardships he went through, by seeking to connect and unite with his fellow man. He became unstoppable in his honesty with himself and others, in efforts to bring about peace and freedom. In fact, although he recently died, he still can't be stopped – his vision lives on.

We all have the ability to be immovable and unstoppable in this way, and we don't need to change a country in order to do it. We just need to have a desire for happiness, freedom, and empowerment, more so than the desires for the exhilaration of aggression or the comfort of avoidance. It starts with the little things: deciding to see how we feel, rather than just believing what we're told; choosing to act with compassion, even when we feel like retaliating; being honest and truthful, even when it would be so much more comfortable to lie; taking responsibility for our emotional state, even when we want to put the responsibility on someone else.

When we live with integrity, we are breaking the cycle of all the inner and outer conflicts that hold us back from living the life we want. It's not an easy practice, but the sense of connection and inner fortitude it brings is well worth the effort.

CHAPTER 4:

THE ESSENTIAL PRACTICE OF PATIENCE

In the last chapter, we talked about using self-reflection and re-sensitization as practical steps for building our integrity, and to start with the little challenges we face. However, what do we do with the big challenges? When we've followed our health program diligently, and we feel like we're making progress but then step on the scale and are shocked to see that we have gained weight, how do we prevent the downward spiral of frustration? What can we do when we're talking with someone, and what they say triggers us so intensely that we can't find a way to respond with honesty and compassion? How do we handle situations that are causing us pain and seem to be out of our control?

The practice of patience is essential for optimal health because it is the key to dealing with the big challenges of life. It is damage control for integrity – meaning it is the practice we must go to whenever we can't find a way to be honest and compassionate. It is a very simple practice, and easy to understand, although it is very challenging to apply because it takes courage, as well as a desire to grow that is stronger than our desire to stay where we are.

DESCRIPTION OF PATIENCE

Without the practice of patience, the problems we face in challenging situations are escalated into much bigger obstacles than they need to be. In other words, when we lack patience, we make mountains out of molehills.

> **Whereas generosity helps us to let go of obstructions, and integrity helps us to not create new obstructions, patience helps us to not blow our current obstructions out of proportion and make them huge barriers to our progress.**

Many of us think of patience as the ability to endure or tolerate challenging circumstances. Although this may be true, this description of patience is incomplete, and for this reason, we often times mistakenly take avoidance to be patience. In fact, when we say things like "I can only be patient for so long," or "My patience is running out," what we're really saying is that we've been dealing with the situation through avoidance, and we're getting too much of a build-up of energy to be able to do this for much longer.

Avoidance brings about tension, so there's a limit to how much we can avoid. Patience, on the other hand, helps us to be more at ease, so we never run out of it. If we are truly practicing patience, we gain more ability to be patient over time, rather than less.

So, what exactly is the practice of patience?

Patience is a movement inward to a place of stillness, and relaxing with our uncertainty in that stillness.

Patience and avoidance are both inward movements of energy, which is why they are often confused with each other. However, with patience we are becoming still and relaxing with that energy, and with avoidance we are not. This apparently slight difference is the

> *reason why patience is a useful tool, and avoidance is*
> *a hindrance.*

Uncertainty is very uncomfortable for most of us. When things don't go according to plan, the way we are expecting them to go, it can bring up a lot of fear. Oftentimes it gives us a sense that we are not in control of our lives, as well as feelings of helplessness when it comes to doing anything about it.

When we let the fear of uncertainty get the better of us, it can have a very significant impact. It can cause us to feel powerless when it comes to cultivating our health goals, it can cause us to lose faith in the idea that we could ever have the type of relationship we truly want, and it can cause us to settle for a livelihood that is far less than what we dream about.

In order to live a life that is increasingly more joyful and fulfilling, we must find a way to deal with uncertainty – other than by trying fight it or to get away from it. The practice of patience is the way to do this.

THE INEVITABILITY OF UNCERTAINTY

The desire to cultivate the practice of patience arises when we realize that *uncertainty isn't going anywhere – it is here to stay.*

This may not sound appealing, but we have to realize that if life was always certain, if nothing ever changed, if things always went according to plan – life would be incredibly stagnant and boring.

Life is a constant flow; it is always changing. The famous saying, "This too shall pass," is a powerful statement that points to the impermanence of life – that nothing stays the same. The constantly changing nature of life brings uncertainty, which is why we oftentimes resist and fear change. However, *change is also necessary for growth and transformation*, and overcoming our fear of the uncertainty it brings is what allows this growth to occur.

The greatest periods of growth I've experienced in my life have always come during the times when I've faced my strongest fears.

One of the biggest sources of suffering I've experienced in my own life surrounds issues I've had with jealousy and possessiveness. With just about every girl/woman I've been in a relationship with in the past, I had a fear that they would cheat on me, even though in most cases there was no logical reason for me to think they would. As a way to avoid the fear of this uncertainty, I would grasp for control in any way I could. For example, if a girl I was dating wanted to go to a party, I would try to make sure I was going with her. Even if I didn't want to go, it was more comfortable than sitting at home and imagining scenarios that would put me into an intense state of anxiety. Of course, the problem with this was that I wasn't really dealing with my issues; I was just looking to make the situation more certain so that I would be comfortable. Because of this, my tendencies toward jealousy and possessiveness didn't decrease over time; instead they caused a breakdown in many of those relationships because I was too dependent on my partners to be able to truly get close and intimate with them.

Throughout the years, the suffering I experienced became so great that I eventually had enough. I knew that I had to take a different approach, because I couldn't live the rest of my life this way. So I started to loosen the reins – when my girlfriend wanted to go to a social event that I didn't want to go to, I sometimes decided to *not* go with her. I was very reluctant to do this at first, because it was very unfamiliar and brought up a lot of fear. During these difficult times, I would lie down, close my eyes, and make an effort to really feel into my body – to feel the tightening in my stomach, to feel the heaviness in my chest, to feel the pressure in my head – and just breathe and relax into stillness with these feelings. They would usually dissipate within a minute or so, and I would continue doing this each time the feelings arose. What I found was that the more I felt into my body like this, the less my mind raced. This caused my emotions to become less and less intense over time, and my mind to gain a greater clarity. I came to realize that my jealous tendencies really had nothing to do with whom I was dating, or whether she was trustworthy – they had everything to do with me not feeling complete and whole within myself.

Fast forward through several years of practicing patience – that girlfriend that I first started doing this practice with is now my wife. I don't depend on her for my happiness any longer, and we know an intimacy that is unlike anything I've ever experienced in any of my past relationships.

Am I completely free of jealousy?

Not entirely. Remember, this is about progress, not perfection. She goes to plenty of social events without me, and although it rarely brings up insecurities for me at this point, every once in a great while an imagined scenario will pop into my head. However, the emotional trigger is nothing at all like it used to be – now I notice it more with a sense of amusement than anything else, because I know it isn't real. The important thing is that although it isn't intense anymore, I still take notice of how I feel, so that I can re-lax and become still with any subtle fears that might be lingering.

This is an example of one area of my life where the practice of patience has brought incredible growth and transformation. I got through the initial fears, which are always the most diffi-cult, and once I did this it was just a matter of staying with the practice as the fears became less and less intense.

Courage is facing our fears. Patience is courage that lasts forever.

In my struggles with jealousy, I gradually stopped trying to control the things *I can't* control, and by doing this I have gradually gained more control of what *I can* control – my mental and emotional state.

DEALING WITH UNCERTAINTY

In essence, there are two general ways that we can deal with the fear of uncertainty. The effective way is through pa-tience, which is often painful in the short-term, but cultivates more long-term empowerment and freedom. The ineffective way is through trying to control the circumstances that are surrounding our uncertainty, as I was initially doing with my jealousy issues. Trying to control our circumstances can bring short-term comfort, but in the long-term it only brings more disempowerment and suffering.

The way we seek to grasp for control is by creating expectations in different areas of our lives, and becoming attached to these expectations. This is why we oftentimes become upset when things don't go as we expect them to. On the surface, we seem to be upset at someone or something else that is disturbing us, but really it's our own attachments that are the source of our suffering. We are trying to control things that we really don't have control over, and on those occasions where something makes us aware of this, it doesn't feel good.

The more we let go of our need for control, the less we create attachments and expectations, and the more we are able to fully accept and embrace the people and circumstances of our lives, just as they are. This leads to more desirable circumstances than any grasping for control can give us.

We all have experienced interactions with someone where both people got frustrated or angry. I know that during those times where I've slipped up and was not practicing patience, my first inclination has been to try to solve the problem – to fix things immediately. Leaving things unsettled can be very uncomfortable, so I would make an effort to come to resolution, even though we were both still angry. In most cases where I took this approach, I only escalated the problem and made it worse. Things that were small disagreements would turn into full-blown arguments, and would last for days or weeks, rather than minutes or hours. In essence, I would end up getting a result that was the opposite of what I was seeking.

> **"One often meets his destiny on the road he takes to avoid it."**
> **- Master Oogway (Kung Fu Panda)**

Once I started to let go of my need for certainty, and therefore not expect or try to force an immediate resolution to frustrating interactions, I got into the habit of taking a "time-out" and feeling into my body, and relaxing into the physical feelings that came with my anger. What I found was that my anger began to dissipate more gradually and naturally, without my trying to force it out through some quick solution. My relationships dramatically improved the more I did this, and I've been able to handle challenging situations with much more composure and equanimity because of it.

The practice of patience is a powerful tool for dealing with personal struggles such as jealousy and possessiveness, anxiety and depression, resentment, anger and frustration, as well as with the struggles we have in our interactions and communications with others. Now let's take a look at how a lack of patience breaks down our physical health, and how the practice of patience helps us to make real progress in improving it.

GRASPING FOR CERTAINTY WITH OUR HEALTH

As I mentioned earlier in the book, my country is incredibly unhealthy. The reason this is the case, and the reason we have been declining in our health for so long is because, as a whole, the underlying issues surrounding our health are not being addressed. One of these underlying issues is that as we have become further removed from nature, and more entrenched in a fast-paced, stimulation-based, convenient way of living, we have become less sensitive to our bodies. And the more we lose touch with our bodies, the more we depend on our minds to obtain "outside" information for the answers to our problems. This underlying issue, as we now can see, is an issue of *integrity*.

The vicious cycles brought about by this lack of integrity have cultivated the wide variety of imbalances and *dis-ease* that we experience today. Naturally, our minds don't like these imbalances (which is ironic, because our problems started by being too focused in our minds to begin with) and so they grasp for control in order to bring us back to balance. They grasp for certainty. However, this grasping further exacerbates our lack of integrity, because it puts even *more* emphasis in our minds, rather than in our bodies by developing sensitivity – and so our problems persist.

How do we prevent our own progress in our physical health, by grasping for control? In what ways do we seek certainty, and end up sabotaging ourselves because of it?

Several years ago, I was working with a woman on both her exercise and nutrition. Everything was going well, but then one day she completely went off her program, and in the following days ended up sabotaging all the progress she had previously made. When I talked with her later about what happened that day, I found out that she had woken up and realized she had more energy and felt better than she had in years. She couldn't remember the last time she felt that good! She got really excited by this, and figured she must be making progress, so she ran to her scale to see how much weight she had lost.

She had *gained* a pound!

She was shocked, and in an instant her excitement transformed to frustration and depression. *In her mind, weighing herself was the only way of measuring progress that mattered – she didn't recognize the feeling of increased energy as progress; it held no credibility for her.* She lost hope, and immediately abandoned everything she had been doing. Once I heard this story, I started having conversations with other clients and realized that many of them were also emotionally dependent on what their scale said each morning.

Over the years, what I've found is that many of us sabotage the progress we make in the very act of measuring it. It's not that the measurement itself is the problem; it's *our expectation surrounding the measurement* that is the problem. We get so fixated in our heads, trying to make sure that everything is going the way we think it should go, and when it doesn't, we become impatient and start on a downward spiral that not only disrupts our progress but actually moves us in the other direction.

For the most part, the problem is that we expect our progress to be linear, as illustrated in the chart below:

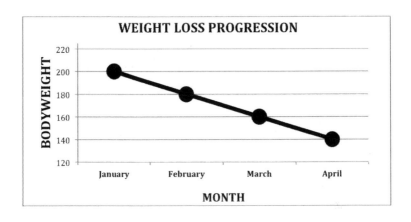

FIGURE A

This chart shows the ideal path of progress; what we all dream of – moving smoothly and consistently from our starting point to our goal, without any challenges or setbacks. We reach our goal, and everything is great!

For the most part, the health industry feeds into our expectations for this ideal progression through its marketing messages:

> *Lose 30 Pounds In 30 Days!*
> *Two Weeks to A New You!*
> *Flat Abs Now! Take The Fast Track To A Lean, Sexy Belly!*

We all know that the above statements are very common – we can pick up any mainstream health magazine and find plenty more that are just like them. They are strong statements that seem to be full of excitement and promise. The reason they are exciting is because they appeal to our desire for an ideal progression. These statements are all basically saying the same thing – "You can now rest assured, because our product will get you to where you want to go, and it will do it quickly!"

The problem with this, however, is that progress doesn't usually go this way – at least not naturally, and the more attached we are to this ideal path, the less likely we are to make the *long-term* progress we really want. In every case I've ever seen, both with myself and with people I've given health guidance to, progress has always had fluctuations to some extent or another. Just as in nature, or in any other area of life we could look at, there are always ups and downs.

Most of us, however, do not want to experience the "downs," the low points that that are a natural part of progression – we want the "ups" without the "downs," because the "downs" bring up fears that maybe we aren't doing as well as we thought, such as in the example above of the woman weighing herself. The "downs" bring uncertainty.

Our inevitable "downs" or low points in life bring great opportunities for growth, but we can only take advantage of these opportunities through the practice of patience.

Rather than accepting that there will be ups and downs, and taking the opportunity to practice patience during our low points, most of us just try to avoid the low points altogether. We grasp for control by becoming attached to an ideal path of progress, and then we go even further and try to create certainty around the activities that would bring about this ideal progression.

How do we try to create certainty around our activities?

Here's one example: Counting calories.

Counting calories and measuring out specific portions of food has become very popular in our society. It takes away all uncertainty, so why wouldn't it be? It's simple math, after all – if we consistently take in less calories than we expend, we can be absolutely certain that we will continue to drop the pounds – we can be certain that our progress will be linear.

Many people use calorie-counting and "point" systems, and are able to follow them strictly enough that they do, indeed, have the linear progress they desire. However, their success is usually not long-term success. The vast majority of these people gain the weight back, and in many cases end up even more over-weight than when they started. Why is this the case?

Programs that rely solely on measuring input and output would only have widespread effectiveness if we were machines.

As far as I can tell, we are *not* machines! We have feelings and emotions, aspirations and desires, and we are not always pre-dictable; even though some of us are very analytical, none of us are entirely mathematical. However, when we try to follow a program in a strictly mathematical way – meaning we rely solely on the scale to tell us how much progress we are making, or determine the effectiveness of our workouts by how many minutes we exercised, and we judge whether or not a food is healthy for us based on the number of calories it has – we are behaving as if we are simply a machine. I remember seeing a hotdog in a bun that was shaped like the box it came in. This hotdog was full of chemicals, and was one of the most unnat-ural-looking pieces of food I had ever seen. Yet, this food was considered healthy, in the nutrition program it was a part of, because it fit within a certain point range for a meal. This type of thinking has had major consequences on our health, as our society is now experiencing.

The issue isn't that "measurement methods" are intrinsically bad or ineffective, and I'm not suggesting that we swing completely in the other direction and only work on body sensitivity. These tools can be very effective if used properly, and if we are in a place in our lives where we really feel that using them will be beneficial for us, then we should use them. Just remember that the wise approach is in the middle of thought and feeling. If we want these methods to truly be effective, then we must be willing to practice patience when things don't go as we expect them to, and we must use them *in conjunction* with our efforts to become more in touch with our bodies throughout the process. If we don't do this – if we use them with the idea of getting easy results without making any effort to grow and develop ourselves in the process – then instead of being tools, they will become a hindrance to long-term joy and fulfillment.

MEDICATING OURSELVES

Regardless of how much we rely on "measurement methods" to remove all possibilities of pain and fear, they still find ways to come into our experience. When this happens, rather than use the practice of patience to move into the pain, and to breathe and relax in the midst of it, we usually follow mainstream thinking – we find ways to dull the pain. When we have a stomachache, for example, most of us don't try to just *feel* the discomfort, and become still and relaxed with it. Even though this practice, over time, could bring insights into lifestyle changes we could make to improve our wellbeing, we just end up taking a pill that covers up the symptom, alleviates the discomfort, and teaches us nothing. When we have a frustrating day at work, rather than feel into it, we meet up with our buddies at the bar for a few beers. When we get our hearts broken, we eat ice cream and watch movies all night to avoid having to feel the ache in our chest.

Common wisdom tells us to just medicate ourselves – in a multitude of ways. As we can see, however, this isn't really wisdom – all it does is provide a quick fix that alleviates the surface of the pain, but does nothing to get to the root of it and bring long-term change. And it does nothing to help us cultivate the type of progress that we want in our lives.

Sometimes we *do* need to medicate ourselves, especially if we are experiencing pain that is so severe that it impairs our ability to function. However, other than in these circumstances, if we want to truly experience progress on a very deep level, we must do the opposite of what we've been conditioned to do, because we know that this hasn't brought long-term growth and fulfillment. We must develop the practice of patience.

FINDING OUR CENTER

Throughout this chapter we've looked at the negative effects of trying to control our circumstances in order to prevent uncertainty, and avoiding our pain by numbing it. We can now see that we create suffering for ourselves when we become attached to a linear progression, and then try to force this progression to occur by using methods that aren't natural for us.

> *Interestingly enough, when we stop trying to force progress, and instead practice patience during the inevitable times of fear and uncertainty, we are then able to really start making the long-term, significant progress we truly want – naturally!*

The reason patience helps us to do this is because it helps us to more clearly find our center. Our center, in essence, is our emotional baseline; it's that place right in the middle of our emotional high points and low points; it is a place that becomes more familiar to us as we become less overly-excited by the "ups" and less overly-upset by the "downs" of life. Take a look at the following image:

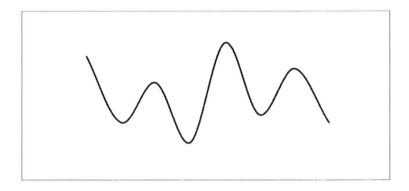

FIGURE B

This image shows what our emotional journey is likely to feel like when we don't practice patience. It applied to me with my jealousy, for example, when I would get overly fearful during uncertain circumstances, and then drastically swing in the other direction and become overly relieved and cheerful when circumstances became stable again. If we look deeply enough into many of our challenges, we will find that it applies to them as well. We develop spending patterns that reinforce the excitement of instant gratification, but then we feel that much more frustrated when we don't get what we want. We immerse ourselves in entertainment that overstimulates us, causing our jobs and other aspects of our daily lives to feel all the more stagnant or boring. We have problems with yo-yo dieting, upswings and downswings in our relationships, and addictions of all kinds.

When we swing way up and way down like this, it is very difficult to know where our center is. This is why I didn't make progress with my jealousy for all those years – I was way too up and down, I was disoriented, I was on a turbulent roller coaster ride that never stopped – I was too unstable with my drastic swings to be able to get a handle on where I actually was, and what it would take to make real progress.

When we start to apply the practice of patience, and continue practicing it, our emotional journey through life begins to transform. Our low points gradually aren't so low – our fears become less intense. Likewise, our high points aren't as high – we aren't as dependent on them for our happiness. With persistent practice, our emotional journey can eventually feel more like this:

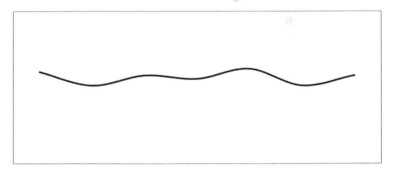

FIGURE C

In the beginning of the chapter, I said that when we don't practice patience, we make mountains out of molehills. When we compare this image to Figure B, however, we see that when we *do* practice patience, *we make molehills out of mountains!*

Over time, our ups and downs are no longer so frequent and intense – they become more gradual and mild. We begin to live life more like a dolphin swimming smoothly through the ocean, rather than that turbulent roller coaster ride we were on before, that felt like it would never end.

Now that our journey is more mild around the edges, it is much easier to get a handle on where our center is:

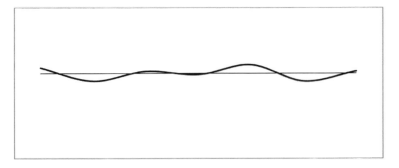

FIGURE D

Living more closely to our center brings great empowerment into our lives, because it shows us much more clearly what we are cultivating now, and in what ways we have been holding ourselves back from living the life we truly want. Until we start to live more closely to our center, we don't have this clarity, because we can't learn it – we can only know it through direct experience. I've talked with many people over the years who told me they knew exactly why they were unhealthy, and exactly what was holding them back from cultivating their health goals. They didn't *know* – they had ideas. If they *really* knew what was holding them back, it would no longer be holding them back. Finding our center through the practice of patience helps us to know, and put ourselves in a position of power to move forward effectively.

When I started the practice of patience to help me with my jealousy, it wasn't the first time I was making efforts to resolve this issue. I had tried many things before, such as reading self-help books, talking with counselors of various kinds, and doing "emotional clearings" of past events. None of these things helped me to see a significant improvement with my jealous tendencies, or the suffering I was creating for myself through them. It wasn't until I started to move toward my center, through the practice of patience, that I realized that my problems weren't stemming from my past – they were being cultivated through the way I was living my life right now. I began to see that it was in the little things, the subtle ways I was trying to control circumstances, the tendency to resist facing my fears that was keeping my jealousy alive.

When we begin to find our center, through the practice of consistently relaxing into stillness with our low points, we are able to gain clarity on our problems in a way that gathering knowledge and guidance from others can never give us.

I only let go of a little bit of control in the beginning, as it was very scary. Even so, relaxing into this little bit of uncertainty started to bring me a little closer to my center. As this happened, I started to get a slightly better grasp than I ever had before of the freedom that was possible for me to experience in a relationship. *I had been told about it, but now I was actually experiencing it for myself.* I wanted more of a taste of this freedom, so this inspired me to let go of some more control, even though it was still scary, though not as scary as before – and this, over time, allowed me to get even closer to my center than I already was. I continued to practice patience in this way, and live my life closer and closer to my center. Then, one day, I realized that jealousy was no longer this huge monkey on my back that I had no control over. My mountains had become molehills that I could easily deal with, and I realized that the initial pain I felt when I first started practicing patience is well worth the long-term joy and fulfillment I am able to experience now, because of it.

If there's one thing we can be certain of, it's that life is uncertain. Challenges and painful circumstances can pop up at any moment, suddenly and without prior notice, and they can bring about fear and discomfort inside of us. We can fight this uncertainty, we can try to manipulate it, and we can try to hide from it, but none of these will actually get rid of it. The more we resist it, the stronger it becomes, and the more long-term suffering we cultivate for ourselves. It is only when we stop resisting it and start embracing it, by relaxing and becoming still with it through the practice of patience, that we are really able to do anything useful with it. When we do this, challenges are no longer a hindrance, but a blessing. Instead of holding us back, they are the doorway to greater growth and transformation.

CHAPTER 5:

THE ESSENTIAL PRACTICE OF INSPIRED ACTION

In the last chapter, we addressed the big challenges in life. We saw how we gain clarity on these challenges and grow from them through the direct experience of finding our center – and we find our center by consistently practicing patience during our "low points." In this chapter, we will now look at using the practice of patience during the "high points" in life, and how this helps us to become inspired and take actions that actually *raise* our center. Living a healthy life – a life that is increasingly more joyful and fulfilling – occurs through the process of raising our center, and continuing to raise it. The essential practice of taking inspired action is the way to do this.

NOT JUST "ACTION" ALONE

Becoming truly effective at cultivating our goals is very challenging for many of us. One of the biggest reasons for this is because we have such a strong emphasis on the actions we need to take, but not nearly as much emphasis on the energy behind how we take them. We don't realize that *the way* we take actions is just as important as the specific actions themselves. Unless we understand how to truly take effective, powerful action, we end up becoming excessively busy or excessively sluggish – both of which are ineffective at helping us to cultivate our goals and live a healthy and fulfilling life.

Taking action alone is not the key to successfully cultivating our goals. Taking *inspired* action is the key. Let's now take a closer look at what inspired action actually is.

DESCRIPTION OF INSPIRED ACTION

To be *inspired* is to be alive; just as to be *expired* is to be dead. Our actions can either be powerful and effective, if there is a strong living energy behind them, or they can be weak and ineffective, if there is not.

> **Inspired action is action that begins from an emotionally charged stillness, and moves outward with the energy of life itself.**

In the last chapter, we saw that patience and avoidance are very similar, but with one big difference – patience ends in *stillness*, and avoidance does not – rather it builds up an inner storm of irritation, anger and resentment that is waiting to come out. In the same way, inspired action is similar to aggression in that they are both outward movements of energy. The difference between them, however, is that inspired action *begins* in stillness, whereas aggression begins with the inner storm that was built-up through avoidance.

> **Patience is movement into stillness.**
> **Inspired action is stillness into movement.**
> **Like the foot that's landing and the foot that's lifting off, both are needed to move us forward.**

Becoming excessively busy occurs because our actions are not coming from a place of stillness. We become so busy that we lose sight of our center; we lose sight of why we are doing the activity to begin with – and we end up becoming busy for the sake of being busy.

Excessive busyness is a form of aggression, and it makes our actions very unfulfilling.

On the other hand, becoming excessively sluggish occurs because our stillness does not come from a place of action. We rest and rest and rest, and become so stagnant that moving into activity feels like it would take an enormous effort.

Excessive sluggishness is a form of avoidance, and it makes our inaction very unfulfilling.

When we combine the practices of patience and inspired action, both stillness and movement – inaction and action – are able to become fulfilling, and from there, wonderful things can happen.

BUILDING MOMENTUM IN OUR PROGRESS

We all know how amazing and full of life we can feel when we are inspired. We hear a touching story about someone who perseveres despite great obstacles, we attend a high-energy church service, or we go to a motivational seminar, and we feel infused with vitality and power. Challenges that seem insurmountable become weaker and less intense in the face of inspiration. We feel stronger, more capable, more determined – we get a glimpse of our immovable and unstoppable nature.

When we become inspired, our creative abilities open up. We are able to see options and avenues we can take that we don't normally see. When we take actions from this place of inspiration, we feel that what we are doing is really making a difference. We are not caught up in the excessive busyness of the rat race, and we are not entrenched in the excessive sluggishness of our living room couch – we are making progress, and we feel good about ourselves while we are making it.

However, inspired action only happens for most of us for very brief windows of time. The reason for this is because, *in most areas of life*, we don't realize how powerful it can be to periodically take a break and move into the stillness of our feelings, and how this can actually help us to build momentum in maintaining inspired action. Rather, we take actions based on an over-emphasis of thought – what we *think* we need to do. When we take action because we *need* to, rather than because we are *inspired* to, our creative abilities begin to close down – we become more rigid. The more rigid we are, the fewer options we can see for ourselves, and the less effective our actions become.

Things don't have to stay this way. We can make changes; we can cultivate new patterns that will allow us to take inspired action much more frequently, and this in turn will allow us to live much more joyfully.

I stated earlier that we don't realize the power of periodically moving into the stillness of our feelings in *most* areas of life. The reason I said "most," and not "all," is because there is one area of life where we do, indeed, see the power of combining patience and inspired action very clearly – sports.

Imagine for a moment that you are a basketball fan, and your favorite college basketball team is heading to the championships.

What will happen in the days leading up to the big game?

They will have a pep rally – they will get everyone together and get them excited about school pride, team spirit, and being the best. They will leave the pep rally feeling pumped up for the game to follow.

Now fast-forward to game day...

The game is about to start, and suddenly the lights go out in the arena. Then all of the sudden there are strobe lights flashing, and an announcer is yelling to the crowd and calling out the names of the players as they run out onto the basketball court. Everyone is cheering as the team huddles up, arms locked as they jump up and down and yell out words of encouragement to each other.

Now the game is in progress...

At a certain point, our team begins to play badly. Shots aren't going in, there's a lack of communication between the players, and the energy level of the whole team becomes deflated. What does the coach do at this point? That's right – he calls a timeout to get everyone re-grouped and back on track.

What do the pep rally, opening show, and timeouts all have in common?

They're all acts of patience – an inward movement into stillness. However, they seem different from the examples we looked at in the last chapter because in these ones we are practicing patience with our high points, rather than our low points. In these examples, a "high point" is intentionally introduced through moving speeches, words of encouragement, recognition, or any other means that would be inspiring for the players. While this "high point" is occurring, the players are not taking action – they are still, and they are becoming emotionally charged in this stillness. They are then sent back into action from this more inspired place. We don't have to be sports fans to see that getting the players inspired before the game is going to increase their chances of winning. Likewise, when the players become uninspired and are playing badly, it's easy to see that if they don't call a timeout and get themselves re-aligned and inspired again, the results can be disastrous.

It's very easy to see the importance of combining patience and inspired action when it comes to sports. However, even though we don't have thousands of fans watching us, it's still just as important for us to cultivate this cycle when it comes to living our life in a successful and fulfilling manner.

Let's take our physical health, for example. When we're reading a magazine while walking on the treadmill, because we're bored and can't wait for it to be over, or we're on a nutrition program that feels restricting, but we follow it anyway out of a sense of obligation, we are like a team that is playing badly, and no time-out is being called to get us back on track – our chances of winning are minimal.

So how do we become inspired while eating, exercising, and following a health program? How do we cultivate our goals, and feel more and more energized and alive throughout the process of cultivating them?

PRACTICAL STEPS FOR CULTIVATING OUR GOALS

In essence, there are two practical steps for cultivating our health goals in a truly effective and fulfilling way. The first step plants the seed in fertile ground, and the second step brings the energy of the seed out into the world.

STEP #1: Bring the Goal to Life through the Dance of Generosity and Integrity

Bringing the goal to life is about getting clarity on what we really want to cultivate – on what our goal *actually is*. When we feel frustrated or stuck in our life, it's usually for one of two reasons – either we don't know what we really want, or we have ideas but we aren't clear on how to go about cultivating them. Many of us expend so much energy trying to figure out the right path to take and the right things to do, but we make our efforts without having real clarity on why we are doing it in the first place. This leads to *uninspired* action. In my experience, when we truly have clarity on our goal, the path reveals itself. We don't have to figure it all out; we just have to get clear on what we really want.

How do we get clarity on our goals? By changing our focus. Wherever we direct our focus is where we will have clarity. If we focus on our problems, we will have great clarity on what we *don't* want in our life anymore. To get clear on our goals, however, we must shift our focus to what we *do* want to cultivate, rather than on what we are trying to get away from.

Our mind is constantly asking itself questions and giving itself answers. This is how it works and how it helps us to function in everyday life, and it does this so much that we usually aren't aware of it. For example, if you aren't sure that you agree with this, your mind will ask "Is this true? Do I agree with this?" It will then search through its catalog of experiences in order to give itself an answer. Our focus is determined by the types of questions we ask ourselves, and if we want to change our focus, then it's important that we change the nature of our questions.

When we feel uninspired or stuck in our lives, it's because we have gotten into the pattern of asking disempowering questions. Here are a few examples:

- Why is this happening to me?
- Why can't things be easier?
- Why do I keep going through the same thing, over and over again?

- Why is losing weight so difficult?
- Why are relationships so frustrating?
- Why is there never enough time in the day to get everything done?
- Why can't I control my temper?
- Why am I always so tired?
- Why can't I get past this depression?
- Why do I have such a hard time getting motivated?

When a question begins with "Why..." or "How come..." it is usually a disempowering question. The reason for this is because when we ask ourselves "Why?" we are trying to make sense of the past. This puts our focus on the past, which keeps the past alive and causes us to repeat it. *(Exception: Why is this important to me?)*

So, what does an empowering question look like? Here are a few examples:

- What do I really want in my life?
- What am I grateful for?
- How could my challenges be a blessing, and how could I grow from them?
- How can I be of service to others in a way that brings me joy?

- If my physical health were to improve, what would that look like?
- If my relationships were to improve, what would they look like?
- If my livelihood were to improve, what would that look like?
- If I wanted to be happy right now, what could I be happy about?
- How can I bring more joy into my life?
- How can this get any better?

These types of questions are oftentimes more difficult to answer when we first start asking them, because finding an answer causes us to redirect our focus and start looking at things differently than we are accustomed to. It may not seem readily apparent, but when we make the effort to transition from disempowering to empowering questions in this way, we are practicing *generosity.* Empowering questions help us to separate ourselves from the past; they help us to part ways with it. By asking questions that get us focused on what we want, we stop fixating on what we don't want – we are able to generously give it away.

I remember writing out a bunch of empowering questions and posting them all over my house, several years ago. I did this so that they would be right in front of my face, and continually reminding me to direct my focus toward what I want. For a couple months I didn't notice any positive changes, because my habit of asking disempowering questions was so strong. Over time, however, these questions gradually started to give me a better sense of what I wanted in my life, and the direction I wanted to take. My goals became more clear, they became more real, they gained *integrity*.

The more we practice *generosity*, by asking empowering questions, the more clarity we get on what we want, which strengthens the *integrity* of our goal.

It's important that we take the time to really participate in this practice and shift our focus. When we shift our focus, we shift our life. By consistently asking empowering questions, we generously let go of past patterns and gain clarity on our goal. Eventually, the integrity of our goal becomes so strong that we are *compelled* to take action on its behalf. We are no longer reading the magazine out of boredom, while walking on the treadmill. We are taking action because we want to take it – because we are *inspired* to take it.

STEP #2: Help the Life of this Goal to Blossom through the Dance of Patience and Inspired Action

Through the gradual application of Step #1, we eventually have an emotionally charged goal with the energy of life dancing inside it. Step #2 is about taking actions that allow this life to express itself – for the inner dance to become an outer dance.

Expressing the life inside our goals begins with patience. We can become incredibly inspired and excited through the process of going through Step #1, but this initial excitement will not last forever, it will eventually diminish – *unless* we continue to reinforce it. The consistent practice of patience adds fuel to the fire of our goals, so our inspiration doesn't burn out.

It's easy to stay on autopilot and go through the motions of our everyday routine – to get out of bed and brush our teeth, eat our breakfast, check our messages, and go to work – all without taking a moment to become still and center ourselves. However, if we take the time to become still, to really feel into why we are getting out of bed, why we are taking action to begin with, it makes a huge difference in the effectiveness of what we do.

The first part of Step #2 is to develop the habit of practicing patience in the beginning of each day, and *then* moving into inspired action. One way we can do this is by writing down our goal on a piece of paper or a note card, and reading it to ourselves every morning when we wake up. However, we don't just read it – we take a moment to really become still and feel into its emotional charge. Then, having taken the time to *feel* inspired, we get up and move into action.

The second part of Step #2 is to practice patience for brief moments throughout the day, whenever we need a boost of inspiration or are facing challenging situations. Otherwise, our actions can become dreary and exhausting. In the same way that a sports team takes timeouts to re-group, so that they don't continue to play badly, we should take timeouts to become still and re-energized, so that our actions can continue to be effective.

> *A friend of mine is a great example of this. He was struggling financially a few years ago, and he found work that had great promise, but it was very much out of his comfort zone. So, whenever his work got challenging for him, he would pick up a picture of himself as a child being held in his father's arms, and look at it. His father had worked hard his entire life to support his family, and my friend*

was very determined to support his father in his later years. So he would look at this picture during challenging moments, and tell himself "this is why I am doing this." This not only helped him to persevere through hard times, it also helped him to feel inspired on a regular basis. He is now one of the happiest people I know – and incredibly wealthy. His father is very well taken care of.

One of the most effective tools that I use to practice patience when I begin to feel uninspired is to imagine that today is the last day of my life. I came across this idea when I saw a video of Steve Jobs giving a graduation commencement speech at Stanford University. I know that thinking about death may sound morbid for some – it's definitely not a practice for everyone – but the thought that this is the last day of my life helps me to really become clear on what my priorities are right now. It strips away everything that isn't essential, it gets me focused on what's truly important, and it helps me to really get to the heart of why I'm taking action. When I imagine that this is the last day of my life, I become very determined to be as helpful and of service as I possibly can for the time that I have, and then I move into inspired action.

Most of us don't think to practice patience in combination with inspired action, to cycle back and forth between them throughout our day, so it may take some getting used to. Fortunately it's fairly easy to do, if we are willing to put in the initial effort to form this new habit-pattern. It's like riding a bike – the first few pedals take effort, but after we gain some momentum it becomes much easier.

Find ways to become still and emotionally charged about your goal that work best for you, whether it's reading your goal, looking at a picture of your family, thinking about your death, watching a video of an inspirational speech, reading a few pages of a personal development book everyday, or any other way that appeals to you. There are no right or wrong ways to practice patience, as long we do it in a way that inspires our actions.

A MOTHER'S SURPRISE

Early in my personal training career, I was very fortunate to be able to train a young woman named Maria. Working with Maria helped me to make a very important discovery – there are some people out there who are so determined to cultivate their health goal, that nothing can stop them. It doesn't really matter how good or bad of a trainer I am, it doesn't matter how big or little the obstacles, these people are going to cultivate their goal, period – and they will either do it with my guidance or *in spite of* my guidance.

Maria was one of these rare people. She was an exchange student who came to the U.S. from Greece, and when I met her, she was about 70 pounds overweight. One of the first things she told me on our first encounter was that her mother was flying out to visit her in about 8 months, and she wanted to lose the extra weight so she could surprise her mother when she picked her up at the airport.

Maria didn't lose a lot of weight for the first couple months that we worked together. She was very out of shape, and would get tired very quickly. However, she stayed persistent because she was so inspired, and her strength and endurance steadily improved. What kept her going was that she found incredible joy at the thought of losing the weight, then reuniting with her mother at the airport and seeing the look of surprise on her face. She envisioned this scenario on a regular basis, and she would excitedly talk with me about it every time I trained her. She also talked with her mother on the phone regularly, which was very energizing for her because she never gave any hint that she was losing weight, working with a personal trainer, or had even joined a gym.

The amount of excitement she had made it feel like she was planning a huge surprise party, rather than trying to lose weight!

After several months of training, Maria's physical conditioning was good enough that her inner excitement started to express itself outwardly. Her improved strength and endurance gave her the ability to take even more action, which she *joyfully* did, and she started to lose weight very quickly. On the days when I wasn't training her, I would walk by the cardio area and see her on the treadmill or the elliptical machine. She didn't read magazines, she didn't watch TV; she just put on her headphones, put a smile on her face – and she *moved!* I could tell that she was truly enjoying the experience because she was so inspired.

Maria's story is a great example of how to integrate the four essential practices that we've discussed so far. Her reason for wanting to lose weight was greater than herself – she *generously* wanted to bring joy to her mother's life. She was also very focused on what she wanted to cultivate, which allowed her to *generously* let go of what she *had* been cultivating. The thought of giving this gift to her mother was very exciting and inspiring for her, which gave her even more clarity on what she wanted, and increased the *integrity* of her goal. She didn't let this excitement fade – she reinforced it through daily acts of *patience*, by feeling into the excitement of her goal, and talking with her mother regularly. Lastly, she took action from the stillness of this excitement – which means her actions were *inspired!*

Maria was immovable in her love for her mother; nothing could move her away from the desire to bring her mother joy. She was unstoppable in her determination to cultivate her goal; no challenges or hardships could sway her to give up. Not only did Maria more than cultivate her goal, she became one of the fittest people in that entire gym. She later told me that when she went to pick her mother up at the airport, her mother didn't recognize her at first.

When she finally did, she cried with joy for 15 minutes.

CHAPTER 6:

THE ESSENTIAL PRACTICE OF MINDFULNESS

In the summertime, the river is generous. It parts ways with some of its water, as it is heated into vapor and given to the sky. Its integrity is cultivated in the autumn season, however, as the water is brought back together again – the river receives rainfall and grows stronger. Winter is the time for patience – the river slows its movements down and becomes still, as it freezes over. In the springtime, however, it is inspired to melt out of the stillness and move, once again, into action.

While these essential practices make up the long cycle of the seasons, they also make up the smaller cycles within it. Cells, molecules, atoms, and sub-atomic particles are continually moving apart, coming together, becoming still, and bursting forth into movement again.

However, throughout all these seasons, throughout all the big-scale and small-scale transformations that the river goes through, the river remains a river.

This river is mindfulness.

DESCRIPTION OF MINDFULNESS

Although the essential practice of mindfulness is the fifth practice that we are discussing, it is a bit different in that it isn't really a separate practice from the previous ones that we've discussed. It is *the essence* of all the previous practices; it is their common thread. In fact, the only way we can truly implement the previous practices is if we are being mindful. In other words, if we aren't practicing mindfulness, we aren't able to truly practice the other ones either. That is how important mindfulness is. In the same way that the river gives a flow to the water droplets that make it up, mindfulness gives a flow to each of the previous practices.

So, what is the practice of mindfulness?

Practicing mindfulness means that we are giving our attention to the direct experience of this moment.

That is it – it is a very simple practice. In fact, it is so simple that we tend to overlook it, thinking that other practices are more important. We underestimate it, because we are so used to looking for complex solutions to our complex problems, that one as simple as mindfulness doesn't appeal to us. We don't see how something so simple can have such a profound impact on our lives.

However, not only can it have a profound impact on our lives, it can have *the most profound* impact. In fact, it is precisely *because* of its simplicity that it is able to have a profound impact.

Of all the practices I've used in my life to cultivate my health, nothing has had as much impact on me as the practice of mindfulness.

ALTERED STATES

For most of my life, I've had a desire for extraordinary experiences and altered states of consciousness. I believed that if I could move deeply into altered states, states that weren't common in my normal, everyday life, I could have the big breakthroughs I was looking for, and life would be amazing.

And *I have* experienced altered states. I've had times when I was meditating where I felt like I was being stretched, like my head was miles above the rest of my body. Other times my meditation would make me feel incredibly light, like my body was ethereal and made up of particles of air. Still other times I would meditate myself into a state of euphoria, which would sometimes last for several days at a time.

Yes, I have experienced altered states of consciousness many times in my life, and some of these experiences *have* brought me insights, some of them *have* allowed me to see things I wasn't able to see before. However, these altered states never really changed my life in the ways I was hoping they would. I never really had the big breakthrough that completely changed everything, and made everyday life really joyful and fulfilling. In most cases, the opposite happened – after the initial euphoria faded, I had a harder time dealing with everyday life. It wasn't until I started practicing mindfulness that I was able to start processing the insights I experienced in these altered states, and live them in my everyday life.

In the beginning of the book, I shared with you the vision I had that inspired me to write it – the vision of being born, and the star exploding. As you can probably imagine, I was in a deeply altered state of consciousness when I had this vision, and it came to me spontaneously while I was meditating. However, there is more to this story than what I've shared so far. Here's the continuation…

After having this vision of our immovable and unstoppable nature, I was in a state of awe. I felt that I was beginning to see the fundamental essence of all of existence, the simplicity that underlies all the complexities that give rise to our problems, and it was amazing. I felt that all the meditating I had done over the years was finally paying off, and I had a strong desire to apply what I was receiving in a way that could help others who are struggling, who feel disempowered, restricted and unhappy, and don't know what to do about it. I was very excited about this idea, and I was very motivated to take action.

However, this feeling of awe only lasted a few days. After that I became very ungrounded. I had all these insights swimming around in my head, and although they were incredible, I didn't know how to piece them together in a way that could be clearly communicated to others. More importantly, I didn't know how to bring them into my own life, how to live them on a day-to-day basis. I felt a greater sense of purpose, but I also felt stuck. I didn't know where to start. This got me frustrated, and then it got me depressed.

After a couple months of feeling depressed, I started to realize how ungrounded I had become, and I knew that I would not be able to make real progress in my life while feeling this way. So, I decided to get some help. I met with a meditation teacher and described the visions I was having, and how I was meditating, and she got me to completely change the way I was going about my meditation practice.

Rather than encouraging me to seek out altered states, my teacher stressed the importance of experiencing this moment in a more *unaltered* way, in a more pure and natural way.

She taught me to keep my attention on this moment, while practicing seated meditation – to feel the act of breathing, the actual physical sensations of the air moving in and out of my abdomen, and to be aware and open to whatever I saw, heard and felt, but not to hold onto any of it. She taught me how to bring this mindfulness practice into my everyday life – how to just be present with whatever I was doing. When I would ask her about my visions, and how I could start living this newfound purpose, she'd tell me to let go of all that for now — to just focus on being present, and the rest would take care of itself.

Letting go was not easy for me, but I made great efforts to do what she was guiding me to do. I dove into this mindfulness practice, both in sitting meditation and in my everyday life. I even started attending retreats at her center, where we would sit in meditation for extended periods throughout the day. I became more and more grounded throughout the process of making all these changes, and I started to be able to deal with life much more effectively, and much more joyfully.

Then, after a few months of mindfulness practice, something interesting started to happen. I would be mindfully washing the dishes, and all the sudden I would get a flash of insight about how my vision applied to washing the dishes. Then I would be mindfully eating and I'd have another flash of insight. Then I would have other insights while mindfully driving to the store, or listening to a friend, or taking out the trash, or exercising, or brushing my teeth.

I started to see how this vision applied to my everyday life, because I was *putting my attention* on my everyday life.

The more I focused on the here and now, and practiced mindfulness in my everyday life, the more grounded and clear I became. I previously had only the belief that there was nothing I needed to achieve in order to be happy, but now I was beginning to experience this firsthand, and life became much more joyful and fulfilling because of it. The puzzle pieces of my vision started to put themselves together, and they were doing it on their own, without any effort on my part. As I continued the practice of mindfulness further, and saw the picture more and more clearly, I realized that all the patterns I had recognized in my health career could be simplified down to six essential practices. Shortly after having this insight, I began to write this book.

THIS UNALTERED MOMENT

One of the greatest insights I had, through my mindfulness practice, had to do with altered states of consciousness themselves. What I realized is that there is much more to altered states than just euphoria, visions, and other extraordinary experiences. Anytime we alter this moment, by adding to it or taking away from it, we are in an altered state of consciousness. For example, if I go for a walk on the beach, but my mind is racing with everything I have to do later on today, I am in an altered state of consciousness. I am focused on my thoughts of the future, which means I am adding them to the experience of this moment, and by doing this I am also taking away from the direct experience of this moment, because while my attention is preoccupied with my thoughts, I am less aware of the feel of the sand on my feet, the salty smell of the ocean, and the breeze touching my skin. I have altered this moment in many ways, and because of this I am not purely experiencing it, or fully appreciating it.

Anytime we add our past conditioning or future concerns to the present moment, we are also taking something away from it as well – our attention. In essence, we are multi-tasking, and when we live our lives this way, when our attention is divided, we waste energy, we are less productive with the time we have, and we are less effective at dealing with our life circumstances.

Most of us seek out altered states of consciousness because, without realizing it, *we are usually in* altered states of consciousness. It is what we are familiar with, and so it is only natural that we continue this pattern by seeking out more intense versions of what we are already experiencing.

The answers to our complex problems, however, are not to be found in more complexity. They are to be found in the simplicity of life. The more we get into the habit of mindfully walking on the beach, or eating, or turning a doorknob, or whatever else we may be doing, the more clear our minds become, and the more our concerns for the future will begin to work themselves out – without our struggling to find the answers.

In the beginning of the book, we talked about a new paradigm for health – one that looks at health as a *process that is cultivated*, rather than a *state that is achieved*. We looked at how the more we focus on states, by putting our attention on the past and the future, the more obstacles we create for ourselves. We also looked at how the more we focus on the process, *by being attentive to the direct experience of this moment*, the more we are able to let these obstacles go, which allows us to flow with life. Life becomes much more fulfilling when we are flowing with it, and although to outside appearances it can look like we are achieving things we didn't have before, inwardly we know that we are merely cultivating what we've always had, and allowing it to blossom.

Mindfulness is the practice that puts us in the process; it's what allows us to flow with the inevitable changes of life, and handle them more effectively. Let's now look at how the practice of mindfulness does this by going through each of the previous practices, and seeing how essential it is to each of them.

THE MINDFULNESS OF GENEROSITY

Imagine it's your birthday, and we are having a party! Your best friend walks in the front door, with a present in her arms, and comes over and hands it to you. She looks directly into your eyes and tells you how much she appreciates your friendship, how much she loves you, and gives you a big hug.

How does this feel? Pretty great, right?

Now imagine that the same scenario happens – your best friend walks in and hands you the present, but there's one big difference – she's on her cell phone the entire time.

This changes things, doesn't it? Even though she is physically handing you the same exact gift, it doesn't feel as sincere, it doesn't have the same energy behind it, and so we aren't as joyful about receiving it.

> **Mindfulness shows us that the power of generosity is not only in the gift itself – which is a specific, concrete state. It is also in the *way* we give, it is in the *process* of giving.**

When we eat a nutritious meal, we are giving a gift to our body. However, mindfulness determines how well the body will receive this gift. If we mindfully give our attention to the process of eating, and eat our food slowly and thoroughly, the body will receive it well – it will break the food down in a way that allows it to be absorbed and assimilated very effectively. On the other hand, if we are not mindful, and we eat our food in a hurried and distracted manner, the exact same gift, the exact same meal, will not be received nearly as well. If we are distracted and hurried enough, a meal that would otherwise bring great benefit could cause stomachache, bloating or indigestion instead.

When a friend wants to talk with us about something they are dealing with, we can give them a gift. We can sit down with them and let them share what is on their mind. However, the way we give this gift will have a huge impact on how it is received. On the one hand, we can be mindful – which means we are paying attention, we are listening to them, and we are seeking to understand what they are going through. If we mindfully listen in this way, we are truly practicing generosity, and they will appreciate it.

On the other hand, we could go through the motions of sitting down and facing them in the same way as above, but without being mindful. We could become distracted by thoughts, and lose track of what they are saying. We could hear something we disagree with, and then start to inwardly build our case for how we will respond, all the while missing the rest of what they are saying. We could periodically glance at the TV while they are talking, causing them to feel that we aren't really interested in what they have to say. There are any number of distracted or unmindful things we could do that would change the entire feel of the interaction. Instead of being grateful for our gift of sitting down with them, they may end up feeling neglected, frustrated, or even angry, and wishing they had never asked to talk with us to begin with.

> **Mindfulness is what gives the practice of generosity its energy, its power, its life. Without it, we are just going through the motions – and the true power of generosity is never in the motions themselves, it is in the sincerity and love that *underlies* the motions.**

Not only does the practice of mindfulness bring more power to our generosity, it also gives us deeper insights into our intentions for giving, which help us to see where our giving might not be as pure as we thought it was. Most of us do not give in a completely pure and generous way all the time. We have subtle attachments and expectations for desired outcomes that we are many times not aware of, because they are below the level of our conscious awareness. The more we practice mindfulness, however, the more these subtle impurities come to the surface – which means we can then deal with them more effectively, and make bigger breakthroughs than we otherwise would be able to do in an unaware state.

THE MINDFULNESS OF INTEGRITY

Mindfulness is essential to the practice of integrity, because integrity only occurs when we are mindful of both our feelings, and our thoughts, words and actions. If we are not mindful of our feelings we are in avoidance; if we are not mindful of our thoughts, words and actions, we are in aggression. There can be no integrity without mindfulness in both of these areas. Likewise, we can only move into aggression or avoidance when we become unmindful, when we move out of the flow of the present moment.

Life is always changing, and this moment is constantly transforming. However, we usually don't experience the freshness and the newness of this moment because we are adding baggage to it. We make our experience of it impure by adding our past conditioning and attachments, as well as our future expectations to it. Adding our baggage to the present moment in this way causes us to take our attention away from it, and this clouds our perception.

We don't experience the world as it is, we experience it as *we* are. However, the more we practice mindfulness, the more we take our baggage out of the picture. This clears our perception and allows us to experience more of the world as it truly is.

Imagine you're at a get-together with some friends. One of your friends walks up to you and says, "That sure is a lot of food you're eating!"

If you are not mindful, if you are adding things to this moment, then you are likely to get offended by this comment, and become reactive or defensive. This friend may have taunted or criticized you in the past, so you add this past conditioning to the present moment, and make assumptions about why he would say this. You may have had problems with unhealthy eating in the past, so you add this baggage to the present moment and feel the need to defend yourself. You may have come to this get-together with the idea of connecting with this friend, and his comment caused you to become upset because it ruined your expectations. All of these things that you add to your experience end up clouding your perception of the newness of this moment, and prevent you from being able to respond in an honest and compassionate way – from a place of deeper understanding and integrity.

However, if you are mindful of the present moment, and not adding anything extra to it, your response can become much different. His comment may have been innocent, with no cruel intentions, and by paying attention to how he says it, by noticing his facial expressions, body language, and tone of voice, you may recognize this and not blow things out of proportion. This allows you to respond in a much more light-hearted way. On the other hand, he *may* have very well meant to criticize you. However, through the practice of mindfulness you may notice that your friend looks very stressed out, or you may be able to intuitively grasp that he has been having a hard time in his life. This may help you to realize that his comment isn't really about you, which can make it easier for you to be compassionate in your response.

The practice of mindfulness helps us to realize that there is always more to the circumstances of our lives than what we see on the surface. The more we pay attention, the more honest and compassionate we become – the more we naturally practice integrity.

Mindfulness not only helps us to effectively practice integrity, it also helps us to realize more quickly when we are not practicing integrity – when we are moving into aggression or avoidance. Oftentimes, the beginning stages of avoidance, and the building up of tension that it brings, can be very subtle and can go unnoticed. By the time we realize we have been building up tension, we have probably been doing it for quite a while. Likewise, it can also be very difficult to tell when our built-up tension is going to tip over into aggression. Our angry outburst can seem to come out of nowhere, and surprise even ourselves.

The continued practice of mindfulness helps us to become more and more aware of when we are moving into avoidance. This means that we begin to notice the build up of tension earlier in the cycle, and are more quickly able to catch ourselves and change the pattern before it builds momentum. Similarly, we also become more aware of when we are going to move into aggression. By noticing that we are getting closer to our tipping point, we are able to pause and try to work with the built-up energy, to move into patience with it, before an angry outburst occurs.

Through the practice of mindfulness, we are able to lessen the influence that our conditioning, attachments and expectations have on our lives. We stop adding more to this moment than there needs to be, and we stop taking attention away from what is right in front of us. The more we practice mindfulness, the less we react to situations with deceit or defensiveness, and the more we are able to respond with honesty and compassion.

THE MINDFULNESS OF PATIENCE

Not only is mindfulness important for the practice of patience – mindfulness essentially *is* patience. The only difference between them has to do with uncertainty. Patience is about paying attention to the feelings that are arising in the present moment, due to uncertainty, and mindfulness is about paying attention to the present moment, regardless of whether there are feelings of uncertainty or not. Basically, patience is mindfulness for the challenging times – whether these challenges are painful with our low points, or exciting with our high points.

Patience can be very difficult to practice because it is much easier to distract ourselves with comfort and security, as a way to hide from our pain, than it is to relax and move into it. However, through the practice of mindfulness with the little things in our daily lives, with the things that aren't painful or uncertain, two very important things begin to happen that help us to deal with the bigger challenges.

The first is that we strengthen our ability to focus our attention. This means that we become less and less distracted in our daily lives, as we strengthen our "awareness muscles." If we aren't mindful in our daily lives, then when uncertainty arises, we are likely to move right into distraction without even realizing it. Through the practice of mindfulness, distractions become less and less common, so when we *do* become distracted, we are able to realize it more quickly, and move back into mindfulness again.

The second thing that happens through the practice of mindfulness is that we become more accepting of change and uncertainty. When we aren't adding anything to this moment, we become more open to whatever experience it may bring, and we are then able to experience this moment in a fresh and new way. This moment that we are experiencing is, by its very nature, one of continuous change and uncertainty. Mindfulness helps us to not be so fearful of uncertainty, and to even start embracing it, because we are living with it more often in our everyday lives. By re-patterning our experience of uncertainty in this way, it helps us to practice patience more willingly when circumstances call for it.

THE MINDFULNESS OF INSPIRED ACTION

The practice of taking inspired action occurs when we intentionally introduce a high point into our life, allow this high point to get us emotionally charged, and then move into action from this place of inspiration. Mindfulness is essential for this practice of taking inspired action, because it determines how emotionally charged and inspired we can become from our high points.

Imagine that you wake up in the morning, turn to the night table at your bedside, and pick up a note card that has your goal written on it. Then you begin to read it. If you are mindful – if you are really attentive to the process of focusing on your goal and getting to the heart of why you really want to cultivate it – then reading this goal will have the ability to get you very emotionally charged, and ready to move into inspired action. On the other hand, if during the process of reading your goal you are distracted and thinking about what you are going to have for breakfast this morning, or concerned about all the things you need to do throughout the day, then reading this same goal will not have nearly the same impact on you. It won't get you emotionally charged, and it won't bring about action that is inspired.

In the last chapter, we looked at how a basketball team introduces high points by periodically taking time-outs to get refocused and inspired during the game. Mindfulness applies in that example as well. The coach could call a time-out, gather everyone together, and give the most encouraging, inspiring talk that the world has ever heard. However, it won't do anything to inspire the players if they aren't paying attention and listening to it. They could sit there in the huddle and hear the words coming out of the coach's mouth, but if they are distracted – fixated in the past, upset over that horrible call the referee made – they are likely to come out of the time-out just as uninspired as when they came into it. It is only by paying attention, by being mindful, that the players can become emotionally re-charged by the talk, and ready to go back into inspired action.

In order to take inspired action consistently and on a regular basis, we must develop the habit of introducing high points in the beginning of the day, and throughout the day. As we talked about earlier, we can do this in many ways – reading our goal, going to websites like www.ted.com and watching short inspirational videos, reading a few pages of a personal development book, imagining that this is the last day of our life, and so on...

However, just introducing these high points isn't enough. We must also introduce them in a way that makes them powerful, and we do this by being mindful while in the process of introducing them. Through the practice of mindfulness, our high points are able to truly bring about an emotional charge, and inspire us to take action.

HOW TO PRACTICE MINDFULNESS

Now that we see how essential mindfulness is for living a healthy and fulfilling life, and how fundamental it is for each of the previous practices, let's look at the two main ways to practice mindfulness:

1. Practicing Mindfulness in Everyday Life

Practicing mindfulness in our everyday life is simply about doing whatever we are going to do, and doing it to the best of our ability. That's it. We perform our activities with as much awareness as possible, rather than in a distracted or absent-minded way. It doesn't mean we are trying to stop the mind, or slow it down – rather we are making efforts to not *divide* the mind. When the mind becomes divided, through multiple points of focus, it creates inner struggle and wastes energy. This causes us to suffer and prevents us from flowing with life. When we practice mindfulness, we are making an effort to give our *undivided* attention to this moment.

This, however, does not mean we are avoiding anything that has to do with the past or the future. If we want to set plans for the future, this is fine – we should just make an effort to be fully engaged in the process of planning, just like we would if we were eating, running errands, or playing with the kids. Whatever we do, we make an effort to do it with awareness, as skillfully as we can, to the best of our ability.

Mindfulness is a simple practice, but this doesn't mean it's easy. We live in a fast-paced, high-stimulation society, so there are many things to distract us from the present moment. For most of us, making an effort to live mindfully is drastically different from how we have been living, so it's important that we are gentle with ourselves as we make this transition. We *are* going to get distracted, our attention *is* going to become divided at times. It's better that we understand and accept this from the beginning, because becoming impatient or beating ourselves up for getting distracted is not going to do anything productive for us. The most effective way to practice mindfulness is to be fully engaged in this moment, to the best of our ability, and when we notice that we've become distracted, we gently bring our attention back to the experience of this moment. With persistent practice, we become less and less distracted over time, and more and more aware of when we do.

2. Practicing Mindfulness Meditation

As mentioned above, bringing mindfulness into our everyday life is not an easy practice, especially if we've never made efforts to do this before. For this reason, we have the practice of mindfulness meditation to help us. Mindfulness meditation is a great support for the first practice of everyday mindfulness, because it is essentially the same as the first practice, except that it occurs in a more controlled setting. By controlling the setting, we allow the cultivation of mindfulness to feel less difficult and overwhelming than if we were just doing the first practice alone. We are also able to move much more deeply into this moment than we would otherwise be able to, and this can give us a new depth of mindfulness to shoot for in our everyday life.

There are many different styles and techniques of meditation. Meditation that is truly aimed at cultivating mindfulness, however, does not hold tightly to any specific style – it uses a more fluid, process-focused approach. For this reason, I'm not going to discuss the validity of different styles, or claim that this technique is good, while that technique is bad. Instead, I'm going to discuss the way of *approaching* meditation – the process of going about meditating – that cultivates greater mindfulness and allows us to bring it into our everyday lives.

The process-focused approach to mindful meditation begins by controlling the circumstances we are meditating in, to the extent that we feel the need to, and then – here's the key thing – *letting go of more and more control* of that environment as we become more and more proficient in our practice.

There are many things we can do to control the setting of our meditation. We can retreat into a quiet room or wear earplugs, in an effort to block out the noise of everyday life. We can close our eyes to block out all visual distractions. We can listen to a guided journey, or contemplate beauty, or count our breaths – all as ways to direct the mind and prevent mental distractions. Yes, there are many ways to control the setting, and this can be beneficial in helping us to not get overwhelmed, to cultivate mindfulness in more manageable steps. However, controlling our setting is a double-edged sword – it can be detrimental if we become too dependent on a specific way of controlling it.

I remember learning in college that we'll do best on a test if we study in an environment that is similar to the one that we'll take the test in. For example, if we listen to music while studying, we'll do better on the test if we listen to music while taking it. This means that if we can't listen to music while taking the test, we are better off not listening to it while studying either.

The same principle applies to meditation. Our everyday life is the test, so to speak, and the more our meditation is like our everyday life, the more it can have an impact on it.

As our meditation becomes more like our everyday life, our everyday life becomes more like our meditation.

What this means is that we are not just meditating to have a nice, relaxed, open experience of this moment, we are also looking to do this in a way that allows us to bring this attentiveness to the moment into our everyday life. Let's say I am going to count my breaths during meditation, and I do this in a quiet room with my eyes closed. In an environment like this, with such little distraction, I may be able to have a very deep and attentive experience of this moment. However, if most of my everyday life is spent in noisy environments, with my eyes open, then there will be a limit to how much I can bring the benefits of my meditation into it. This doesn't mean that my meditation is not valuable or effective; it just means that I now have an idea of how I can make further progress. Maybe when I'm ready, I can do the same meditation, but move out to the living room, where more of the sounds from outside can be heard. Maybe as I become more proficient in this setting, I decide to open my eyes while meditating. Maybe as I get to the point that I can count my breaths without getting distracted, I drop the counting and just start following the breath instead. The more I gradually let go of ways to control the experience of meditating, the more mindful I can become in my everyday life.

So, how do I get started in the practice of mindful meditation?

Mindfulness meditation has become very popular in recent years, so there are many resources on the subject. Looking through books at the bookstore, or checking out articles or videos online, are easy ways to learn about mindfulness meditation, and find an approach that we are drawn to.

However, once we find an approach that suits our character and temperament, if we want to truly make deep, significant progress, it is best to receive individual guidance from a teacher. Our ego (the solid, rigid sense of who we are) tries to keep us distracted from the present moment, because that is how it maintains control of our lives. The more control the ego has, the more we suffer. This ego is very clever, and finds ways to distract us that we usually aren't aware of. A good teacher – someone who has walked the path of mindfulness deeply enough to know the pitfalls and traps that the ego sets up – can help us to adjust our meditation in an effective way, and with the right timing, when these challenges come up. This can help us to take months or even years off our learning curve – or more accurately our *unlearning* curve.

A good mindfulness meditation teacher:

- Doesn't hold tightly to one style or technique, claiming that it is the best
- Doesn't try to entice us with promises of altered states, special powers or quick fixes to our problems
- Stresses the importance of engaging with life, rather than escaping from it
- Is inspiring, because they are living what they are teaching
- Focuses on empowering us to find our own way, rather than on making us dependent on them.

Everybody has the ability to meditate!

There's one more thing I'd like to discuss about meditation before moving on. Over the years, many people have told me that they can't meditate because their minds are too distracted. I find this interesting, because a distracted mind is exactly why we *would* want to meditate!

The truth is, we all have the ability to meditate. We just need to start where we are, and not expect more from ourselves than we can handle in this moment. We don't need to meditate for hours a day, or with a laser-focused mind, in order to get tremendous benefits from it. When I first started meditating, I had a hard time sitting still for more than five minutes. My mind would be racing the entire time, and I couldn't wait to get up. The only reason I stuck with it is because I had read some books on the benefits of meditation that inspired me. This caused me to give myself a different message. Instead of telling myself that I couldn't do this because my mind was too distracted, I told myself that *it was important for me to do this* because my mind was too distracted. This slight shift in thinking made all the difference, and kept me going. With consistent practice, five minutes eventually wasn't so unbearable, and I moved up to ten minutes, then up to fifteen. For years I meditated for fifteen to twenty minutes a day, and although this may seem like a short amount of time, it still had a big impact on me over the years.

Ultimately, the belief that "I can't meditate" breaks down when one of two things happens. Either we begin to really see that our suffering comes about through our own distractedness, and we become so fed up with this suffering that we let go of our limiting belief, or we become aware of the benefits that meditating can have on our life, and this inspires us so much that we let go of our limiting belief.

Extreme suffering or extreme inspiration – our rigid identities can't stand up to either one of them.

We are all capable of getting into a consistent meditation practice, we just have to want it badly enough. Our only limits are our own beliefs – and a belief is merely a thought that we keep thinking. My hope is that if you didn't previously see how much suffering is brought about by distractedness, or how much benefit we can get from meditating, you see a little more of them now.

ALLOWING THE RIVER TO FLOW

When obstructions arise that block the flow of the river, a number of things happen. In some places, the water pools and becomes stagnant – in this analogy, we feel stuck and unable to make progress. In other places, the water begins to eddy – we're continually moving, but we're going in circles, never really feeling like we're getting anywhere. In some places, the water becomes dammed up and brings a buildup of pressure – we become frustrated because we have all this potential inside us, but we don't know how to release it. Still in other places, the riverbed dries up – we lose sight of our potential, our passion for life withers away, and we feel hopeless.

One of the greatest gifts we receive through the persistent practice of mindfulness is the realization that all the suffering we experience is brought about only by ourselves.

We construct the walls that block the flow of our own lives, and bring about all the varieties of suffering we experience.

We see that by adding the past to this moment, we become rigid in our identity and stifle our ability to grow and change. We see that by adding the future to this moment, we become stressed and anxious about things that haven't yet happened. In fact, most of what we worry about doesn't ever come to pass – we suffer unnecessarily. We realize that being mindful doesn't mean we are free of pain – to be sure, there are times when the experience of this moment is painful. However, we also realize that when we fixate on the pain, when we let our minds run wild with thoughts of how painful this pain is, we bring about suffering that is ten times worse than the actual pain itself. In life, some pain is inevitable; suffering is a choice.

The practice of mindfulness shows us how we hold ourselves back, and then it helps us to break the chains of our self-imposed oppression and not do this to ourselves anymore.

Mindfulness is truly the practice that underlies all other practices. In the same way that we don't see the individual droplets of water that flow through the river, mindfulness brings forth the interconnectedness of all the other practices – the more mindful we become, the more the individuality of other practices begins to disappear. They all blend together into a flowing whole.

Although it is not an easy practice, and it may not seem to be an exciting practice, or a quick fix practice, there is no practice that can cultivate freedom, empowerment, and joy as deeply and as powerfully as mindfulness can. Our immovable and unstoppable nature is alive within us right now, and it is through the practice of mindfulness that we can bring it forth into our everyday lives.

MAKING THE COMMITMENT

There is no way to prove that mindfulness can do everything that I'm saying it can, or that any of the other practices can either, for that matter. In fact, my intention in writing these words was never to give a guarantee to your mind that would make it feel comfortable and secure. Rather, my intention has always been to touch your heart. There is so much more to us than what our minds can see, and my hope is that if you've felt stuck or discouraged in your life, you feel a little more hopeful and inspired now.

If this is the case, if anything you've read in this book so far makes you feel more inspired, then there is only one more thing left to talk about – the importance of commitment. Making the commitment to cultivate a healthy life is the last of the essential practices that we will discuss. It is only through this commitment that we will stay with the other practices long enough for our immovable and unstoppable nature to blossom and bear fruit.

CHAPTER 7:

THE ESSENTIAL PRACTICE OF COMMITMENT

In the last chapter, we talked a lot about flowing with life, but what exactly does it mean to be "in the flow?"

To answer this question, let's imagine a scenario where we are in the flow. Let's imagine we are in a boat, moving down a river with the current. Now that we are in the flow, here is the first question – are we moving the boat, or is the current moving the boat?

The current is moving the boat. When we are flowing with life, it is the same way. We aren't struggling to do the right things

– rather the right things are happening through us. Of course, this doesn't mean that we are just sitting there idly. We are using our oars; we are steering and maneuvering within this flow, with our actions. However, when our actions are going with the flow, they feel very different than when we are trying to paddle upstream. When we think of times when we've been "in the zone," whether it was while giving a work presentation, or in a sports event, or just one of those days where we "woke up on the right side of the bed" and everything was going great, we can recall what it feels like for our actions to be light and effortless, for everything to be aligned and going smoothly.

Now back to our boat. We realize that the current moves the boat, but here's the next question – what exactly *is* this current?

Obviously, the current is moving water, but it is also more than just that. Movement can occur in any direction. In order for there to be a current, however, there needs to be a *unified movement* of water. The water must all be heading in the same direction; otherwise it won't have enough power to bring our boat along for the ride.

Flowing with life, or getting in the zone, means that everything that isn't essential drops away. We are not wasteful with the energy of our life, because we are not in conflict, we are not torn, we are not dividing our focus in many different directions. The more we are living in the flow, the more we are able to have the direct experience of being whole and complete within ourselves. Until we are living in the flow, this concept is just that – a concept. We can logically understand it, but that isn't the same as living it.

One more time – let's go back to our boat. We realize that the current is moving the boat, and we realize that it is able to do this because it is a unified movement of water. Now for the last question – what brings this unified movement of water about? How is the river able to exist as a river?

The riverbanks!

The riverbanks are the container that gives shape to the water, and directs its movement. Without them, the water would spread out in many directions and lose its power. The river is only able to exist because of its riverbanks.

In the flow of life, these riverbanks are commitment.

DESCRIPTION OF COMMITMENT

Just as generosity is the companion of integrity, and patience is the companion of inspired action, so mindfulness is the companion of commitment. Whereas mindfulness is the inner essence of the practices, commitment is the outer container that shapes and directs them.

Without commitment, we won't stay with the other practices long enough for a unified movement to occur, and for a flow to be possible. In other words, we will stop practicing them before they are powerful enough to have a noticeable affect.

So, what is the practice of commitment?

> **Practicing commitment means we are setting an intention, and aligning ourselves more and more with this intention, so that it can have a significant impact on our life.**

It's important for us to understand what commitment is, and how it shapes and directs our experiences. However, it is also important that we understand that commitment alone is not an essential practice of health. We can make unhealthy commitments that bring more suffering, just as we can make healthy commitments that bring more joy and freedom. Our life can flow in ways that we don't want it to, just as easily as it can flow in ways that we do.

It's not just about making a commitment; it's about *what* we are committing to as well.

Our intentions determine what kinds of practices we will gravitate toward, which will determine what kinds of results we will cultivate in our life. For example, a person who has the intention of getting dramatic results, and wants them instantly without having to make any lifestyle changes, will not have gotten very far into this book. They will probably have stopped reading after the first or second chapter. The practices described here won't appeal to them, because they don't align with this person's intention. On the other hand, another person may have tried all kinds of quick-fix solutions over the years, and never got the long-term results they wanted. They may very well be sick and tired of looking for short cuts at this point, and ready for a different approach. The practices in this book may be *very* interesting for this person, because they align with the intention for something deeper. I'm confident that *you* are this kind of person, that *you* are ready for something deeper, because you probably wouldn't have read this far into the book if you weren't!

The sixth essential practice of health is the *commitment to cultivating it!*

Remember our new paradigm for health – health is the process that characterizes how we live all aspects of our life. So, when we commit to cultivating our health, what this means is that we are setting the intention to implement the essential practices of health in every area of our life.

Not in one area of life, not in two areas – in every area!

Have you ever heard about the world-class athlete, someone that was considered to be at the pinnacle of physical fitness, who was physically abusing his wife? How about the man who has an amazing relationship with his wife, but hates his job? How about the woman who has a successful career, and is financially well off, but is overweight and has all kinds of physical ailments?

Just because we excel in one area of life doesn't mean we are living with great joy and fulfillment. We can be completely focused and committed in one area, and even become the best in the world in that one area, and *still* experience enormous suffering, because our inattentiveness to the other areas of our life causes them to crumble.

The commitment to cultivating health means we are not striving to cultivate certain areas of life *at*

the expense of other areas. It means we leave no area of our life behind. *It means we are striving to excel in life itself.*

Commitment gives power to the *intention* that directs the *attention* of mindfulness. When our intention is limited, our attention is limited – and therefore the areas of our life that bring us joy are likely to be narrow. When we set the intention to cultivate our health, however, we are setting a truly great intention, because we then begin to pay attention to *all* of life, and give ourselves a greater ability to experience all of it as fulfilling.

Of course, this doesn't mean that we need to focus on every area of our life equally at all times. It's natural and appropriate to focus on some areas more than others, as the circumstances of our life require. For example, if I am having problems with my physical fitness, and I have a strong desire to improve in this area, then by all means I should make that a strong focus in my life right now. I should focus on it more than other areas, if that is what I intuitively feel is best for me at this time. However, it wouldn't be wise for me to become so fixated on it that I become disconnected from my wife, or I begin to neglect my work. Even if I turn things around and become incredibly strong and fit, if my loved ones feel alienated in the process, or my career begins to break down, it probably won't feel as fulfilling as I had hoped or expected.

THE IMPORTANCE OF COMMITMENT

In the very first fitness center where I worked, there was an extremely overweight woman named Jodi that came in every morning. Jodi worked out everyday like it was the last day of her life. She had the intensity of a high-level athlete, and she consistently showed up everyday. She trained herself so rigorously that just watching her made *me* tired! For the two years that I worked in that fitness center, I watched Jodi train. Surprisingly, however, she never lost any weight.

A few years after I had left that fitness center, I was walking down the street and ran into Jodi. Actually, she had to call out to me as I was passing by, because I didn't recognize her. In fact, she had lost so much weight that even when she told me who she was, I still didn't recognize her for a few moments. Once I got my bearings, I congratulated her on her successful transformation, and asked her how she did it. It turns out that for all those years, after Jodi would finish her workouts, she would walk around the corner to a pizza shop and eat a pizza. Once she started to focus on her nutrition, however, and aligned her eating with her intention to lose weight, she got drastically different results than she had been getting.

When we set a goal, the reason we don't see its immediate cultivation in our lives is because we have conflicting intentions.

The challenges that Jodi had are the challenges that we all have, because we all have conflicting intentions to some extent. We can't get into the flow and make significant progress when we have conflicting intentions, just as water can't become a powerful current if it's moving in different directions. We all know what it feels like to work hard for something and not understand why we aren't getting the results we want. The reason we aren't getting them is because we aren't in full alignment – we are doing things that hold ourselves back, and we usually do this without realizing it.

Commitment is important for two reasons:

1. It takes time to discover where we have conflicting intentions, and which of our habit-patterns reinforce and strengthen these conflicting intentions
2. Once we do make this discovery, it also takes time to transform these habit-patterns or replace them with newly adopted ones that are more aligned with our goal intention.

When I first met Jodi, her behaviors weren't aligned enough with her intentions for her to be able to cultivate her goal. However, what set her apart from most was how *committed* she was to cultivating her goal. Because of this commitment, *she was able to stick with it long enough to realize where she was holding herself back*, and then make the necessary changes that got her more fully aligned and freed her from these limitations.

THE REWARDS AND CHALLENGES OF COMMITMENT

Although the commitment to cultivating our health is the last of the essential practices that we are discussing, it is actually the first practice that we must implement. Just as a river can only form where there are first the right land conditions, the other practices we've discussed can only become powerful, and help us to live our lives more in the flow, when *we* have the right land conditions – when we are *committed to sticking with the practices*. The reason we discuss this essential practice last is because making a commitment is not something we should do lightly. Lightly made commitments rarely last. It was important for us to go through the other practices first so that we could see what we are getting into, before making this commitment.

Let's now go over the other practices one more time, and look at the challenges we may face, as well as the rewards we can cultivate, by committing to them over a long enough period of time.

COMMITMENT TO PRACTICING GENEROSITY

The reward for committing to the practice of generosity is a life of greater abundance.

The conflicting intention that makes this practice challenging is our tendency to focus on "What can I get?"

The practice of generosity is what allows us to live an abundant life. Every time we give in a truly generous way, we are also giving ourselves a message, subconscious at first, that says, "I have something to give, and it feels good to give it." We may not feel the impact of this message at first, but the more consistently we practice generosity, the more it comes to the surface. We begin to change our outlook on life, and on ourselves. When we give ourselves this message frequently and consistently enough, the message itself even begins to change. Instead of saying "I have something to give," it starts to say "I have more than enough to give," and then "I have an abundance to give."

Just like anything else we focus on, the more we practice generosity, the stronger and more capable we become at being generous. As we become more capable in our giving, something starts to happen – we begin to receive more – not because we are trying to get more, but because receiving keeps the momentum going – it strengthens our pattern of being generous and allows us to give even more. This is the reciprocal nature of life.

When this pattern of practicing generosity becomes so engrained that we are in the flow of giving – when our giving is done naturally, with ease and joyfulness – we are living an abundant life.

This is a magnificent way to live, but it takes commitment in order for the practice of generosity to bear this kind of fruit. The biggest challenge to practicing generosity and living in the flow of abundance is our focus on "what can I get?" This focus occurs because we believe that by obtaining or achieving something that we don't have now, we will be happier, or that by giving of ourselves, we are somehow diminished. When we become fixated on obtaining that which we don't have, the message we send ourselves is that the circumstances of this moment are not enough, that something is missing.

Most of us don't realize it, but our focus on "What can I get?" leads to us living with a *lack mentality*.

If we have experienced enough suffering from living in lack, and are joyful at the thought of living in abundance, then generosity is a practice worth committing to.

COMMITMENT TO PRACTICING INTEGRITY

The reward for committing to the practice of integrity is a life of greater intimacy and connection.

The conflicting intention that makes this practice challenging is our tendency to seek short-term comfort.

Integrity is the practice that brings more intimacy and connection into our lives, because through our honesty we are being authentic, and through our compassion we are expressing our desire to connect. Nothing builds stronger bonds, within ourselves or with others, than when we are being real and showing that we care.

The practice of integrity is challenging, however, because we place such high value on personal, short-term comfort. This seeking of short-term comfort is a conflicting intention to the practice of integrity, and brings about much long-term suffering. Look at aggression and avoidance – these are the two components of our vicious cycles, and they arise when we are *not* in integrity. Although one is an excessive release of energy and the other is an excessive build-up of energy, they do have one thing in common – they both provide short-term comfort. Aggressiveness is appealing when it is more comfortable to release our anger than it is to hold it in any longer. Avoidance is appealing when it is more comfortable to keep the peace than it is to get involved in a potential confrontation. Both provide short-term comfort, but both also bring about disconnection and a breaking down of relationships.

Committing to the practice of integrity happens when we see that we are the source of our own joy and suffering, and choose to take responsibility for our lives.

With this commitment, we are able to stay with the practice long enough for our intentions to come into alignment – meaning that our desire to authentically connect eventually becomes stronger than our desire for short-term comfort.

If we have experienced enough of the disconnection and long-term suffering that comes with the seeking of short-term comfort, and are joyful at the thought of building stronger and more intimate relationships, with others as well as ourselves, then integrity is a practice worth committing to.

COMMITMENT TO PRACTICING PATIENCE

The reward for committing to the practice of patience is a life of greater growth and transformation.

The conflicting intention that makes this practice challenging is our tendency to grasp for certainty.

Oftentimes we want growth and transformation in our lives, yet we also grasp for certainty and resist facing our fears. These are conflicting intentions. Growth can only occur when we stop trying to control things so tightly, when we stop focusing on keeping things the way they are. Could the bud express the full glory of the rose, if it kept itself from changing by stifling its natural flow?

The practice of patience takes commitment because we usually aren't aware at first of how we resist change and stifle our own growth. It takes time for this awareness to come to the surface, and the way it comes to the surface is by repeatedly and consistently moving straight into our feelings of fear and uncertainty, whenever they arise, and relaxing in the midst of them. The more we consistently practice patience in this way, the more clarity we gain on how our fears are holding us back, and the more ability we have to conquer these fears.

We can consciously have a tremendous desire for change, and at the same time have subconscious desires and tendencies that prevent this change from occurring.

I've worked with countless people who have had strong desires to cultivate their health goals, and yet would continually do things that sabotaged their progress and kept them where they were. *Whenever we have an issue with self-sabotage, we have an issue with facing our fears.*

When fear arises, the potential for growth also arises.

Once we realize this, we stop looking at our challenges as negatives that are holding us back, and start looking at them as opportunities to develop greater strength and bring about positive change. In order to take advantage of these opportunities, however, we must move straight into the fear that we are feeling, relax in the midst of it, and stay committed to doing this consistently enough that clarity and strength can arise. Growth and transformation don't occur through one or two acts of patience. They occur through the commitment to the *ongoing practice* of patience.

If we have experienced enough suffering from being stuck, and are joyful at the thought of growing and transforming our lives, then patience is a practice worth committing to.

COMMITMENT TO PRACTICING INSPIRED ACTION

> *The reward for committing to the practice of taking inspired action is a life of greater joy and purpose.*

> *The conflicting intentions that make this practice challenging are our tendencies toward excessive busyness or excessive sluggishness.*

Committing to the practice of taking inspired action isn't really needed, in regards to the inspired action itself. Action is easy to take, once it's truly inspired. The real challenge to this practice is in setting up the conditions that allow our actions to be inspired more consistently – *this* is where commitment is necessary.

Excessive busyness and excessive sluggishness are conflicting intentions to the practice of taking inspired action, because when we take inspired action we feel energetic and alive, and in both of the other scenarios we feel the opposite – that our life energy is draining away from us.

So what does the commitment to practicing inspired action look like?

For those of us who are excessively busy, it means conscientiously and consistently making the effort to slow down and get refocused on what our goals are, and why we want to cultivate them – and then move back into action. For those of us who are excessively sluggish, it means conscientiously and consistently feeling into our goals and then making the effort to start – to move into action while we are inspired. It can be difficult to take this initial action, but once we do, it becomes easier to keep going with it.

Changing the habit-patterns of being excessively busy or excessively sluggish can be very challenging. For most of us, these patterns have been deeply engrained into our daily routine for many years, and so they have a strong momentum that keeps them going. Unless we commit to the consistent practice of taking inspired action, by changing up our routine and setting up new habit-patterns throughout our daily lives that reinforce our goal-emotions, the inertia of these long-standing patterns will overpower our efforts.

If we have experienced enough anxiety, depression, or exhaustion from excessive busyness or excessive sluggishness, and we want to change this and start living with more joy and purpose, then setting up the conditions that bring about inspired action is a practice worth committing to.

COMMITMENT TO PRACTICING MINDFULNESS

The reward for committing to the practice of mindfulness is a life of greater freedom.

The conflicting intention that makes this practice challenging is our tendency toward attachment.

True freedom has nothing to do with whether or not the circumstances of our life are favorable. We've all heard of people who are miserable, even though they are surrounded by the nicest things that money can buy, and we've all heard of the opposite – people who have found joy and peace in the midst of challenging or even painful circumstances. Our surroundings and circumstances don't determine how much freedom we have – the only thing that determines that is how much we've let go of our attachments.

The extent to which we let go of our attachments, is the extent to which we experience true freedom.

Here's the interesting thing about our attachments – they always have their source in the past or the future, never in the present. Our conditioning, limiting beliefs, and mental and emotional hang-ups have to do with how we've perceived and processed experiences from our past. Our worries and expectations have to do with our focus on the future. None of these have anything to do with this moment.

The more we live in this moment, through the continued practice of mindfulness, the more these different forms of bondage can begin to drop away. However, most of us, without realizing it, resist freeing ourselves from this bondage. We want to be in the present moment and experience the freedom it can bring, but we also want to hold on to our attachments. These are conflicting intentions, and they make the practice of mindfulness difficult to stick with.

We can't be in the present moment and simultaneously hold onto attachments. The very act of

holding onto attachments keeps us in the past or the future.

Our attachments are familiar, and we hold onto them because they are what we use to define ourselves; they give us a sense of identity.

> *How do we define ourselves? We could all come up with a long list of things that describe our characteristics, and define who we think we are. Some of the things on this list we will perceive to be positive, and others negative. However, whether positive or negative, the things on this list limit us if we hold to them too tightly. For example, let's say that you see yourself as a gentle person. This sounds like a positive trait, and in many cases it is. However, there are circumstances in life where being gentle is not effective. A friend might need a bit of "tough love" to help snap them out of their self-absorbed turmoil, and get them back on track. The children may be showing signs of disrespect and entitlement, and assertively setting boundaries may be the most loving and effective thing we can do to help them in the moment. However, the more strongly we define ourselves as being "gentle," the less capable we become at responding with forcefulness when circumstances call for it. This limits*

us, and causes us to deal with the changing circumstances of our lives less effectively.

This rigid identity that we develop through our attachments gives us a subconscious form of security in our own existence, and this may sound like a good thing, but it comes with a price – it puts us in a box, because we have very clear ideas of who we think we are, and what we think we are capable of. The more opinionated we become about ourselves, the more limited we become in how we deal with life. We become less flexible and adaptive to our ever-changing circumstances, which causes us to live with a sense of lack, become less connected with others and ourselves, feel unable to grow, and feel uninspired. It causes us to suffer.

The only kind of bondage that holds us back from true freedom is the bondage that we put on ourselves.

The practice of mindfulness takes commitment because letting go of our limited views, no matter how much we consciously want to, isn't something that our sub-conscious usually feels secure in doing right away. I know, from firsthand experience, that when we move deeply enough into the present moment, it can feel like we are dying. We aren't actually dying, in the physical sense, but in a way, we *are* dying, because when we move deeply enough into the present moment, we let go of our limited views of who we think we are, and what we think we are capable of. *Who are we, and what are we capable of, when we don't hold tightly to any definitions?*

Through the continued, persistent practice of mindfulness, our attachments and limited views of ourselves have the chance to gradually weaken, and eventually fall away as they are ready to – like ripe apples falling from a tree. Without commitment, we won't stay with the practice of mindfulness long enough for our attachments to become ripe and fall away.

When we hold onto nothing, everything is available to us.

If we have experienced enough suffering from holding onto our attachments, and our limited views of who we are and what we are capable of, and are joyful at the thought of living more of our lives with true freedom – a freedom that nobody can ever take away from us – then mindfulness is a practice worth committing to.

CLOSING ONE DOOR, OPENING ANOTHER

As we can see, implementing the essential practices of health on a consistent basis, and bringing our conflicting intentions into greater alignment, is not an easy path. However, if we truly want to be fulfilled – if we want to live a life of greater abundance, intimacy, growth, joy and freedom – then going through this challenging process of alignment is well worth the effort. Commitment is the essential practice of health that gives us the ability to persevere through our challenges and transformations.

In the next, and final, chapter, we will discuss what it really takes to make this commitment and stick with these practices long enough for them to have a positive and noticeable impact on our lives. Before we move on to this, however, I'd like to address one more thing about commitment: many of us have a fear of it. We don't like the idea of committing – it makes us feel restricted, as if our options are cut off and our freedom is being taken away from us.

I can understand why many of us would fear commitment. From the time we are little children, others have been telling us how we should be living our lives. We are told what is right and what is wrong, what is good and what is bad. We've felt forced to do things we *didn't* want to do, and we've been told to stop doing things we *did* want to do. And it doesn't stop in childhood – many of us, even as adults, feel that others are in control of our lives, and dictating how we should be living it. Because of all these things, many of us feel confined even at just the thought of making a commitment. For just a moment, I want to ask that we let go of our past conditioning around the concept of commitment, and look at it with a fresh set of eyes...

Why do we really have a fear of commitment?

Here's the bottom line: commitment is a tool that allows us to cultivate some things more deeply than we normally would, and other things less deeply than we normally would. What this means is that when we make a commitment, we are cutting off certain options, but at the same time opening up other ones that we didn't previously have access to. There is always a trade-off like this when we make a commitment. If we view the trade-off as favorable, meaning we want the options that are opening to us more so than the ones we are letting go of, we will feel good about the commitment, and it won't feel confining. On the other hand, if what is opening up to us isn't as appealing as what we are giving up, the trade-off won't be favorable, and we will feel confined and restricted.

The reason many of us have a fear of commitment is because in the past, when we've felt pressured or forced to commit to something, we didn't feel good about the trade-off – and so, because of this, we were more focused on what we were losing, on what we were giving up, rather than on what we were gaining.

Our fear of commitment didn't come about because of anything that is inherently wrong with commitment itself – it came about because of *the way we've made commitments.*

I remember watching a scene in the movie *The Matrix* where Keanu Reeve's character, Neo, is in the backseat of a car with Trinity, and they are heading to a secret location so that Neo can meet their leader, Morpheus, for the first time. Neo has a problem with authority, and so when the woman in the front seat starts to give him orders, he opens the car door to get out. Trinity grabs his arm to stop him. Here is the dialogue:

Trinity: Please, Neo, you have to trust me.

Neo: Why?

Trinity: Because you have been down there, Neo. You know that road. You know exactly where it ends. And I know that's not where you want to be.

(Neo ponders this as he looks down the road. He then decides to stay in the car, and closes the door)

A truly powerful and effective commitment can only come about when we *want* to make the commitment – not when we are *pressured* to make it. Neo closed the car door himself; no one made him do it. And when he did it, he was cutting off the option of going down "that road." He didn't feel restriction or a loss of freedom by cutting off this option because the trade-off was worth it – he was willing to give up a road he no longer needed *and* deal with his challenges with authority, all for a chance to meet Morpheus and find answers that he was deeply searching for. If Neo had kept the door to that road open, he would have closed the door to meeting Morpheus.

Making the commitment to cultivating our health will only be effective if we truly want to make it. And the way we want it is by walking down that road – the one called "What can I get?" But we don't just walk down the road – we walk down it enough times that we know exactly where it ends – in feelings of lack. Likewise, we have to have gone down the road called "Aggression and Avoidance" enough times that we know that it ends in disconnection and alienation, and that the road called "Grasping for Certainty" leads to stagnation, and the road called "Busyness and Sluggishness" to being uninspired, and the road called "Attachment" to suffering of all kinds.

When we make the commitment to cultivate our health, we make the effort to stop walking down these other roads – not only because we know where they lead, but also because we don't want to walk down them anymore. Sure, we cut off our options, to the best of our ability, but this doesn't feel restricting or limiting, because the less we walk down these roads, the more we walk down other ones – and these new roads, although they may be challenging at times (especially in the beginning), lead us to areas of life that are much more satisfying and fulfilling.

Commitment is the structure of life.

Ultimately, when we take a close look at what commitment really is, we realize that it is much more than just the decisions we make that direct our lives. On a broader scale, it is the structure that gives existence and flow to life itself. There can be no life, or a flow to life, without structures that support and direct it. What this means is that commitment is a part of our lives, whether we realize it or not. Imagine that I tell you

"I don't like commitments. They make me feel confined, so I don't make them." What am I really saying? What I am saying is that I am so fearful of commitment, that *I am committed to not making commitments.*

This, in itself, is a commitment!

We all make commitments, because we all have preferences and make decisions about how we will behave and conduct ourselves that direct the flow of our lives. The question we have to ask ourselves is not whether we will make commitment a part of our lives or not. It already is. The question we have to ask ourselves is this: Will we make our commitments consciously, with an intention that helps us to dive deeper into freedom and joy? And are we willing to make this commitment, even though there will be challenges, especially in the beginning, with changing our habit-patterns? Or will we make commitments unconsciously, by default, based on what we've already been doing?

If we want to live our lives differently than we've been living them, we must become committed to something different than what we've been committed to so far.

Making the commitment to cultivating your health is not a commitment that you need to make to me, or to your family, or to your friends – it is a commitment that you make to yourself. And you only make it if you really want to.

Are you ready to commit to cultivating your health? Is the trade-off worth it?

CHAPTER 8:

CONCLUSION

THE EXPLODING STAR

The star in the sky is a perfect example of *generosity*. It is always shining, it is always giving of its light, and it never expects anything in return. However, it can't truly give without also receiving, and so the star *does* receive. The very process of giving away its light causes its core to become denser – its *integrity* is strengthened. The star becomes more attractive and gravitationally strong because of this increased integrity, and so it receives objects that are drawn to it from space.

For a very long time, a dance takes place between generosity and integrity. The star continues to give its light, while its core becomes more and more dense. We may look up at the star and think that nothing is changing, that no progress is being made, but it is – it *always* is. Eventually, through the long dance of generosity and integrity, the core becomes so dense that it reaches critical mass, and its progress is no longer invisible. It contracts inward on itself to a place of stillness – it undergoes the great act of **patience**. In the stillness of patience, in that very moment, the core becomes immovable – nothing can disturb it, nothing can shake it. And so, because nothing can move it, because it has such tremendous power within itself, it is then compelled to move outward on its own. Contraction is coupled with expansion, and so the star becomes unstoppable – it takes **inspired action** and projects itself outward, full of energy and life, in all the directions of the universe.

Throughout the entire lifecycle of the star, from birth to explosion and back to birth again, it is also a perfect example of **mindfulness.** It doesn't give its light for a while and then become distracted and turn it off. It doesn't become denser and then take a break to try to interpret and analyze what this increased integrity will do for it. It doesn't reach critical mass and resist the patient movement into stillness, because of fears of what might happen. It doesn't procrastinate about exploding, because it wants to make sure that everything is perfect before taking action. No, it doesn't try to do any of these; it doesn't try to figure things out; it doesn't try to control anything. It just flows through its life with continual awareness, as it flows through the essential practices. It blends them together into a seamless whole. It makes them one.

Lastly, the star goes through its particular lifecycle and explodes because its entire life is shaped and directed by a specific, innate pattern. There is a structure that guides the flow of its entire existence, and the star is **committed**, from beginning to completion, to flowing through this structure. What this means is that when the star is born, it already has the entirety of its existence, from birth to explosion, contained within itself. Every point in its life contains *all* of its life, and so there is nothing new that it needs to gain or achieve in order to explode – it just needs to stay in the flow, committed to its course, and the explosion will unfold naturally.

It may seem that the star's life ends when it explodes. However, this is not the case. The explosion is the blossoming of the goal, it is the immense transformation that occurs through the culmination of a fulfilling process, and it is the beginning of an even greater goal. Through the explosion, the star is able to spread its influence far and wide, and become a part of many other objects throughout the universe – planets and moons, comets and asteroids, humans, trees and other living things. It will even become a part of other stars, and help them to explode in the eternal cycle of life, just as it was formed and guided to explode from the gathered fragments of other stars that exploded before it.

WE ARE EXPLODING STARS!

Just like the star in the sky...

We start this life with commitment! The merging of our mother's egg and father's sperm provides our unique DNA, and this DNA is the structure that shapes and directs the flow of our lives from a microscopic, single-celled organism to a fully formed human being. Truly miraculous!

Just like the star in the sky...

We have an explosion within us! It has been there since the moment we were conceived, and it will be there until the day we die. Our explosion is an explosion of abundance, connection, growth, joy and freedom. This explosion is not inherent in some, and absent in others – it is an innate part of every single one of us!

Just like the star in the sky...

There is nothing that we need to achieve in order for this explosion to come to the surface and manifest itself! All we need to do is cultivate what is already inside of us, and we do this by implementing the six essential practices of health!

Just like the star in the sky...

We can play in the dance of these practices for a long time... and just like the star in the sky, much of our progress is likely to be invisible... and just like the star in the sky, if we stay attentive to the *process*, then the *result* takes care of itself – the explosion becomes inevitable!

Lastly...

When we explode – by losing that extra weight, or freeing ourselves from depression, or transforming our dysfunctional relationships into healthy, more intimate ones, or developing a livelihood that we truly love and are passionate about – we can't help but spread our influence far and wide. Our explosion will inspire others, it will help them to feel more hopeful and empowered, and it will help them to cultivate more fulfilling lives – just as others who came before were able to inspire and help us.

THE BATTLE AND THE DANCE

My friend, we are now coming to the end of this book! A lot has been covered in the previous pages – some of the concepts have been brought forth in ways that are probably very new, while others in ways that are perhaps familiar. All of the concepts, however, do have one thing in common: They all go against the grain of what we, as a society, are doing right now to cultivate our health – whether we are talking about the health of our bodies, the health of our relationships, or the health of our livelihoods. As a whole, we have been seeing a steady decline in the quality of all these areas of life. The practices in this book are the key to turning things around for all of us. However, because these practices *do* go against the established grain, it makes them more challenging to follow – initially. Yet, with greater challenge comes greater reward.

As I've said before, this is not an easy path – it's rewarding, it's fulfilling, but it's not easy. Knowing that we are going to face challenges with these practices brings up the last thing we really need to address:

> *What's the bottom line? What does it really take to commit to these practices, and actually stick with them long enough for them to have a significant impact on our health, and in our lives?*

In my years as a health and fitness professional, I've seen many different kinds of people have long-term success in cultivating their goals – male, female, young, old, introverted, extroverted, people of every shape and challenge. In my own life, I've also cultivated long-term success in various ways – sometimes I've had it by becoming more active, while other times by slowing down; sometimes by fighting with all my might and conquering, while other times by surrendering and letting go.

From what I can see, there are no specific ways to bring about long-term success that will work in every kind of situation, and for every kind of person. What I *have* noticed, however, is that whenever long-term success does occur, there are always two ingredients – two intangibles – that are always present:

Faith and Determination.

Earlier in the book we talked about using the six essential practices of health to turn our battles into a dance. Giving rise to our battles and turning them into a dance is what faith and determination are all about. These two are the foundation for our goals – not just in cultivating them, but also in giving them their existence to begin with. Through our faith, a goal arises, and through our determination, we are able to commit to the essential practices that will allow this goal to blossom.

Living with faith means that we are trusting the inner knowing of our heart. This inner knowing can come as a gut instinct, an intuition, or just a sense that comes from deep within us, and it tells us that there is more to who we are, and what we are capable of, than there appears to be. *When we trust the heart's message, we develop faith, and this faith causes a battle to arise within us – one between the status quo and a new way of being.*

Having determination (or a mind that is not deterred) comes about when we make the choice to reconcile the battle that is within us, and restore harmony. At the same time that our faith gives rise

to the battle, there also arises a determination within us to end the battle – and we end it by embodying our faith, by actually living the direct experience of it in our everyday lives. *With the development of determination, our battle is transformed into a dance.*

What is the difference between a battle and a dance? In a battle, the sides are drawn. There is a clear distinction, a clear separation, between *this* side and *that* side – and these sides are in opposition to each other. In a dance, on the other hand, there are no sides. There is an intermingling of energy, rather than a clear separation. Forces work with each other in a complementary way, rather than against each other in an oppositional way, and they work together so well that it can be difficult to tell where one force ends, and the other begins.

From this description, it may seem like the battle is bad and the dance is good, but that is not the case. If we only danced one kind of dance for our entire lives, we would get pretty bored with it. The battle is an important part of life, because it gives us the opportunity to take part in a greater dance than we were able to before.

How does faith give rise to a battle within us?

To answer this question, let's first imagine what it would be like if we had no faith at all. What would life be like if we saw no possibilities within ourselves for anything greater? What if we believed that we are merely what we appear to be on the surface, that there isn't anything more to us than what is apparent? What if we believed that we are only capable of doing what we are already able to do – that we are capable of nothing more?

When we really imagine this, when we really put ourselves in these shoes, what we find is that when we have no faith, we have no conflict or struggle inside of us either. The reason there is no struggle is because we see no differences between the life we *are* living and the life we feel we are *capable* of living. When we see no difference between the two, we don't make efforts to improve on anything, or to cultivate anything new, because there's no point in even trying. Therefore, because we don't make efforts to transform ourselves, we don't struggle. However, this doesn't mean we are happy or fulfilled – it just means we are *resigned*. This is our "fate" in life, and there is nothing we can do about it.

If we are obese, for example, and this is an area of life where we have no faith that we can change, then we won't even set a goal to lose weight. Maybe we've tried many times before, and because nothing worked we came to the conclusion that our genetics, bone structure, or some other perceived limitation has caused obesity to be our lot in life, and it's just something we are forced to live with. Once we come to this conclusion, we give up, we become resigned to our fate, and therefore we stop making efforts to cultivate something that we no longer believe we are capable of cultivating. We aren't happy or joyful about being obese, but we aren't struggling with it either. We are just resigned. This is life without faith.

Now let's imagine that faith is inserted into the picture. Maybe we meet someone who was just like us – resigned to a life of obesity – but they came across an approach that was completely different from anything they had tried before, and it helped them to lose the extra weight and keep it off! Or maybe we watch a movie, or read a book about someone who seems to be in a hopeless situation, with no way out of it, but somehow they find the strength from deep within themselves to persevere and transform their life! Or maybe it's as simple as reading a statement… a statement such as *"Over-eating doesn't occur because of issues with discipline or motivation. It occurs because of the movement back and forth between aggression and avoidance. It occurs because of an issue with integrity."*

Any one of these situations could spark faith in us, under the right circumstances, because they challenge our beliefs.

They help us to open ourselves up to the possibility that maybe we *are* more powerful than we appear to be. Maybe our issue isn't that we aren't capable, but merely that we've been *misguided* – both in our approach and in where we've put our attention and our efforts.

When we really open ourselves up to these possibilities, we become joyful, and perhaps even excited. This joy, this excitement, is a message from our heart. The message it is giving us is a confirmation that we are, indeed, greater and more capable than we appear to be. When we trust this message, we have faith.

Now, here's the interesting thing about faith – once it arises within us, we can no longer go back to just staying resigned with being obese. The reason we were resigned before is because there was no difference between what we believed we were capable of and how we were actually living our life. Once faith arises, however, we *do* see a difference between them, and so the sides begin to form. On the one side, we have our new vision of what we are capable of cultivating – a slender, fit body. On the other side, we have what we've been cultivating – an obese body.

A slender body on the one side. An obese body on the other. This doesn't line up. There is an imbalance here, and this imbalance brings up a disturbance inside us, which causes our life to become unsettled. This disturbance, this unsettling, gives rise to a goal, as well as a battle.

In this battle, one side – the side that has faith in the inner message of the heart – wants to reconcile the battle by cultivating this greater vision of ourselves, and bring this goal into the actual experience of our everyday life. It doesn't want us to just have an *inner knowing* that this slender body is possible – it wants us to *actualize* this inner knowing, and *directly experience it* for ourselves. This side wins the battle when the slender body of our faith becomes the slender body of our direct experience. Then, once again, there are no sides – our faith and our direct experience are no different from each other.

In the process of winning the battle, the battle has been transformed back into a dance – but it's a greater dance than we were dancing before.

Now, the other side has a very different agenda for "restoring peace" and reconciling the battle. On this side, we find the limiting views we have that cause us to continue cultivating an obese body, as well as all the strongly ingrained habit-patterns we've developed that keep us where we are. This side isn't interested in change; it isn't interested in growth. Our limiting views are threatened by the very idea of any "possibilities" that would help us to break free from our current limits. Likewise, our habit-patterns have no interest in being transformed, and they *definitely* don't want to be replaced. This side is going to fight and resist change all the way, and it will do this through various means. It will try to convince us that our goals and dreams are unrealistic. It will tempt us to listen to those who discourage us, those who doubt our abilities, and those who don't want us to change. It will appeal to our desire for comfort, and tell us that we should just relax for the moment, because we can always start later. It will do whatever it can to keep itself alive, and it will do this by trying to delay or stifle any activity that helps us to cultivate our goals and dreams.

This side wins the battle, and "restores peace," when it has convinced us to lose faith in the inner message of our heart, and to give up on our goal. When this happens, once again, there are no sides. When this happens, once again, we see no difference between what we *could* cultivate and what we *are* cultivating. When this happens, once again, we are dancing – but it isn't a new dance, it isn't a greater dance – it's the same old dance we were dancing before. And the problem with this is that when a dance becomes too familiar, when we are just going through the motions, it really isn't a dance anymore. Our heart isn't in it.

So, which side will win in our battle?

Well, that depends entirely on us and how much faith we have. *And how do we strengthen our faith?* By continuing to listen to the heart's message, and continuing to trust it. The more we do this, the stronger our faith becomes. Fortunately, the heart is speaking to us all the time, through our feelings, so we have plenty of opportunity to strengthen our faith. When we really open ourselves to the heart, then a statement like this...

> *You are a magnificent being, and you are capable of living a life filled with abundance, connection, growth, joy and freedom.*

... will cause a feeling of joy to arise from within us. This joy is a message from the heart, telling us that this statement is pointing toward truth. On the other hand, a statement like...

> *You are weak and powerless, and you don't deserve to be happy.*

… makes us feel bad, and this is also a message from the heart. The reason why the heart gives rise to a bad feeling within us, in this instance, is to let us know that this statement is *not* pointing toward truth, that we are *not* weak and powerless. The language of the heart is the language of feeling. Learning this language takes practice like anything else, but just the awareness of a positive aspect of a negative feeling can be liberating. The heart is always giving us messages, and not just about statements – it's giving us messages about everything. We just have to be willing to receive them, and to trust them. The more willing we are, the more we are able to do this.

The reason a strong faith is so important is because our faith is directly linked with our determination. If we have strong faith in the inner message of our heart, we will have a strong determination to actualize this inner message and bring it into our direct experience. If our faith is weak, on the other hand, then our determination to embody the heart's message will also be weak.

Determination isn't a feeling, like the inner knowing of the heart. It's a choice we make with the mind. It happens when we've had enough of living the way we've been living, and we are ready for something more. We draw a line in the sand, and decide that we are going to align our efforts and our actions with our faith, with the inner message of our heart, and we are going to do this regardless of the challenges – both inner and outer – that come up. Once we have this kind of determination, when it is strong enough that we know we are never going to stop listening to our heart, and we are never going to give up on ourselves, then we don't even have to think about applying the essential practice of commitment – the commitment will arise spontaneously from deep within us, and it will be truly powerful. With strong determination, our commitment to cultivating our goal will be strong enough to help us stay on course until we are able to embody this goal, this inner message of the heart, and directly experience it in our life.

We don't cultivate our goals with the heart alone, and we don't cultivate our goals with the mind alone – we cultivate our goals through the joining of the heart *and* the mind. Each one makes the other stronger, when they work together. We need a strong faith that keeps us rooted in our heart, so that we stay centered in our belief in ourselves, and in our capabilities. We need a strong determination that gives us the inner fortitude to stay on course, regardless of how challenging or uncomfortable it may be to do so at times. A strong determination is important, because the "other side" is very strong. Our limiting beliefs and habit-patterns are no joke. For most of us, they have been around for many years, and they have a lot of momentum in their favor. However, when we have determination, when we decide that we are going to stay true to our commitment, no matter what, then these limiting beliefs and habit-patterns begin the process of weakening and breaking down, and our goal begins the process of blossoming. It may not always happen as quickly as we would like, or in the ways we are expecting it to, but with faith and determination, bringing about a strong commitment to use the essential practices of health, this blossoming is inevitable.

FAITH, DETERMINATION, AND THE SIX ESSENTIAL PRACTICES

Imagine that we have a seed, and we want to cultivate this seed. We want to help it to sprout, grow, and blossom into a flower. Every day we give this seed fresh, clean water, and just the right amount of sunlight. However, there's one problem – the seed was planted in low-quality soil that has been stripped of all its nutrients. *Will the seed be able to blossom into a flower?* Not likely.

Now let's imagine we take a different approach. We plant our seed in fertile, nutrient-rich soil. However, the water we are giving to the plant is polluted, and the sun doesn't shine on this particular patch of land very much. *Will the seed have a good chance of blossoming into a flower under these circumstances?* Once again, not likely.

Only when we plant the seed in nutrient-rich soil, and give it the right amount of fresh water and sunlight, is it able to grow and blossom into a flower.

Faith and determination are the soil that our goal resides in. When they are strong, the soil is fertile, and rich with nutrients. When they are not, the soil is depleted. Likewise, the practices we use are the water and sunlight that we feed our goals with. If our practices are powerful, we are giving our goals clean, fresh water and just the right amount of sunlight. If our practices are weak, we are feeding our goal polluted water and too much or too little sunlight.

Now, if we really look at this analogy, we see that we could be using the most effective practices in the world, but if our faith and determination are weak, we will use these practices lifelessly, just going through the motions out of a sense of obligation, and blossoming will elude us. On the other hand, if we have strong faith and determination, but we use weak practices, then we will keep going and going and going, but never get anywhere. Eventually, our faith and determination weaken, and we give up. Once again, the blossoming eludes us.

It is only when we combine strong faith and determination with powerful practices that our goals can blossom. And here is the beauty of the six essential practices of health – they are the most powerful practices we can use. Throughout this book, I've given practical examples of how they have been used to cultivate goals. I've done this through some of my own personal experiences, through the experiences of some of my health clients, as well as through examples of inspirational figures I've studied. However, I've also given examples of how these practices can be found in other places, like the flowers, the rivers and the stars. Why would I do this? Why is this relevant? The reason I've done this is because I wanted to show that these practices aren't just practices. They aren't just virtues either.

These six essential practices of health are actually the forces of nature!

Yes, they are in the flowers, the rivers and the stars, but they are also in the mountains and the deserts, the oceans and the skies, and the animals and the trees. They are in the smallest particles of matter, and they are in the largest celestial bodies. They are in all of existence. They are in you and me.

We can't go wrong when we use practices that come from nature, because if there's one thing I've noticed over and over again in my life, and finally come to realize, it's that the more we align ourselves with nature, the more powerful we become, and the more we are able to live harmoniously. I've also noticed the opposite – the more we take actions that are out of alignment with nature, the less harmonious our life becomes.

Something amazing happens when we combine strong faith and determination with practices that have the power of nature behind them. They mutually reinforce each other and make each other stronger! Our strong faith and determination give us the ability to commit to these practices, and stick with them. Unlike the many times in the past when we've committed to certain practices and didn't get anywhere, when we commit to *these* practices, we really *do* begin to see changes in our life! With these changes, our faith grows even stronger, as does our determination, and so we dive into these practices even more. We keep going back and forth like this, gradually transforming the battle into a dance, until our faith and determination are so strong that we have an immovable heart and an unstoppable mind, and our goals blossom!

The name of this book is *Immovable Heart, Unstoppable Mind*. When we are rooted in a strong enough faith, our hearts become immovable, and nothing can move us or shake us from our belief in ourselves, or the greatness we have within us.

When our determination is strong enough, our minds become unstoppable, and nothing can hold us back, drag us down, or stop us from cultivating our goals. Lastly, when we use the *powers of nature* with an immovable heart and an unstoppable mind, there is no limit to what we can cultivate.

PERSONAL MESSAGE

My dear friend, thank you for joining me on this adventure of self-discovery! The process of writing this book has truly been transformative for me, and I hope that reading it has been transformative for you as well! I would like for us to finish this book where we started – with *vision*. If you'll recall, in the very beginning of the book, I shared with you my vision:

> *My vision is to cultivate a healthy and fulfilling life, not just for myself but for my whole human family, through an approach that brings abundance, connection, growth, joy, and freedom – for the benefit of all.*

On a fundamental level, this vision hasn't changed for me. I still have the same vision as when I first started writing, and it's still the most amazing one I can imagine living. However, through the process of writing, this vision has gone through many transformations *within me*. It has deepened and broadened in ways that I wouldn't have imagined before I first started putting pen to paper. This book has primarily been focused on individual health – the health of our bodies, the health of our relationships, and the health of our livelihoods. However, throughout the process of writing about these things, I've been flooded with other visions – visions of using the six essential practices to effectively restructure the ways we govern our people; visions of "conceiving" new businesses and business models, similarly to how humans are conceived, and allowing these businesses to grow in ways that align with nature, which will allow them to bring more widespread benefit to society, and to the planet; visions of ways we can build more synergistic communities, so that we can live in greater joy and harmony with each other. The insights and increased clarity that I've continued to receive about how my overarching vision can be cultivated in greater and greater ways has only made it all stronger and more real within me. This has caused me to have even more faith in it, and even more determination to bring it into the experience of everyday life. This is the battle that I've chosen to take up and transform into a dance.

It would be easy for me to look at these visions and just dismiss them, believing they are pie-in-the-sky ideas that could never happen. And I probably would dismiss them if I allowed the limiting views in my head to have that kind of influence on me. Fortunately, I've listened to these limiting views enough times in my life to know that all they do is stifle my dreams, and this doesn't make for a fulfilling life. So, I don't choose to do this anymore. These visions bring a wonderful feeling of joy to me, and I have faith that if my heart is giving me this kind of message, then they are able to be cultivated. However, I also know that the way to do this is not by trying to figure it all out. I don't have all the answers, and I don't try to. I just allow these visions to inspire me, and then I dive into the actions that are directly related to this moment, and I do this with as much presence as I can. I know that as I continue to do this, insights will continue to be revealed, and things will continue to work themselves out.

I know we have some major challenges and struggles going on in the world right now, and these struggles are very painful on many levels. Often, they are so painful that we end up believing that the first order of priority is to change the government, change businesses, change the banking and money systems, and so on. Although these changes are important and must be dealt with, if we want to bring about truly effective change, then the first order of priority must always be the change that needs to happen within ourselves.

The reason this book is focused on individual health is because, as Gandhi said, we must be the change that we want to see in the world. There is incredible wisdom in Gandhi's statement. However, its wisdom doesn't come from it being some deep, esoteric statement; its wisdom comes from it being a simple statement that is aligned with nature. Just look within the body – when we have a diseased organ, it means that the individual cells of that organ are not functioning properly. An organ can only be as healthy as the cells that make it up. This organ can't truly be free of the disease unless the individual cells go back to functioning in a more optimal way. If we try to treat the organ without addressing the cells that make it up, all we will be able to do is cover up the symptoms. When we cover up symptoms, the feeling of discomfort may temporarily subside, but the root of the imbalance is still there, and so is the disease.

We are the cells of this planet, and there are a lot of challenges on the planet right now because there are a lot of challenges *within us* right now. If we want to see the government change, then we need to change the way we govern and direct our own lives first. If we want to stop the pollution and destruction of the planet, then we need to stop the pollution and destruction of our bodies first. If we want to reconcile the strong divisions in power and control that we see in the world, then we must be willing to reconcile the battles within ourselves that create the strong divisions between how we are living our lives and how we want to be living them. We can't continue to look outside ourselves, at the "powers that be," and think that they are the source of our suffering. They are not. As long as we believe that, we will be disempowered, and we will feel like victims. We are the source of our own suffering, and we have the power within ourselves to alleviate this suffering. Making efforts to bring about change on a community level, national level, or global level will only be effective to the extent that we are willing to make these changes within ourselves first.

I am in love with our world, and I'm truly excited about the possibilities of what we can cultivate together. The bigger the challenges we face, the bigger the opportunities for growth, and the greater the dance we can take part in. I know that many of us have made tremendous efforts in the past to bring about change in ourselves, without having success, and I'm excited about the differences we will notice as we apply this same kind of effort with the truly powerful practices that are described in this book. I have seen these practices completely turn people's lives around. I know, because I am one of these people. Throughout most of my life, I have been much more *unsuccessful* with my goals than I have been successful. In fact, for nine years of my health career I owned a fitness and nutrition center, and in that entire nine years I never once had success in "achieving" any of my business goals. I fell into a depression for the last few years of running that business, because I just couldn't figure out what I was doing wrong. That business failed, I went bankrupt, and had my car repossessed. I've also tried to write books at several times in my life. I never got past the first chapter before giving up. I know what it's like to feel miserable, depressed, and disempowered in life.

So what helped me to turn things around? Well, there were several things, but the straw that finally broke the camel's back of discouragement was a simple statement. I heard someone say: "There is nothing to attain." That was it, but that was enough. I had heard statements like this before, but this time something clicked. As soon as I heard it, I had this gut feeling, this strong intuition from deep within me. It told me that this one simple statement was pointing to a truth I had been missing. I realized that because I had the illusion that there was something I needed to achieve, that something out there was going to make me happier, I was subconsciously tying my value up in whether or not I achieved it. This one little realization turned things around for me. I started to have success with my goals, and I also started to get clarity on the practices that brought this success about.

By the time I decided to write this book, it was a very different kind of goal than when I had tried to write books in the past. This time I knew that the book wasn't something I was trying to attain or achieve; it wasn't even something I was trying to create. Rather it was something that already existed within me, and I was merely cultivating it and allowing it to blossom out into the world. Because it has always been inside me, I also knew that by writing this book I would add no more value to myself than I already had, and by failing to write it I would take no value away from myself. In short, by realizing that there was nothing to attain or achieve, I had a greater sense that I was complete and whole within myself, that the source of my happiness and joy came from within myself, and that the results of my efforts wouldn't change this in any way. As I've written these pages, I've stayed focused on the process, on the present moment, living each day as if it is the last day of my life, inspired to give as much as I can with the time that I have, and I've let go of concerns about the result. And in that letting go, I am experiencing great joy and satisfaction in the blossoming of this goal!

The inspiration for this book came about through my love for humanity, the inner greatness and brilliance that I see in all of us, and my desire to help others who are struggling in ways that are similar to the ways I have struggled. What I want more than anything is for this vision to no longer be *my* vision. I want it to be *our* vision. We all deserve to feel abundance, connection, growth, joy and freedom in this life, and we are all capable of cultivating it. If you feel inspired by what you've read, and have gained a greater faith than you had before, then I am truly honored that I could be of service. That has been my intention all along. Let's cultivate this vision together, hand in hand, and let's do it so we can help others to do the same.

Throughout history we have had inspirational figures that we have looked up to, and seen as very different from ourselves. The time for this separation is over – we are now ready to start cultivating the inspirational figures *inside of us* that we have always looked up to *outside of us*. Now we know how to do this. By joining forces, by dancing together, we can make this happen.

We have come full circle, and are back to the beginning of the book. Let's write it again... but *together* this time.

A SUMMARY OF THE 6 ESSENTIAL PRACTICES

PRACTICE	DESCRIPTION	FUNCTION
GENEROSITY	A joyful separation, a joyful parting of ways, that seeks nothing in return.	Helps us to let go of the past and release obstructions without focusing on them. Makes our goals more powerful by giving them a greater purpose than our own self-interest. Brings greater abundance into our lives.

PRACTICE	DESCRIPTION	FUNCTION
INTEGRITY	A unification, a connecting, a coming together, that brings about inner fortitude and strength.	Helps us to not create new obstructions that impede our progress. Lessens the intensity and frequency of our vicious cycles, and the negative consequences that we experience because of them. Brings more intimacy and connection into our lives.
PATIENCE	A movement inward to a place of stillness, and relaxing with our uncertainty in that stillness.	Helps us to not take our current obstructions and blow them out of proportion, making them huge barriers to our progress. In fact, it does the opposite - it turns our mountains into molehills. Brings more growth and transformation into our lives.

PRACTICE	DESCRIPTION	FUNCTION
INSPIRED ACTION	Action that begins from an emotionally charged stillness, and moves outward with the energy of life itself.	Helps us to cultivate more of what we really want in our lives, rather than trying to move us away from what we don't want. Brings more joy and fulfillment into our lives.
MINDFULNESS	Giving our attention to the direct experience of this moment.	Helps to free us from attachments that keep us feeling stuck in our life. It is the inner essence, the common thread, of all the previous practices, and is necessary in order for them to be powerful and effective. Allows us to experience true freedom.

PRACTICE	DESCRIPTION	FUNCTION
COMMITMENT	Setting an intention, and aligning ourselves more and more with this intention, so that it can have a significant impact on our life.	It is the outer container that gives shape and direction to all the previous practices. Gives us the ability to stick with the other practices long enough for our goals to blossom, and have a noticeable affect on our lives.